T0114860

# Comprehension

The
**READING PUZZLE**

## Elaine K. McEwan

### Allyson Burnett
### Raymond Lowery

**CORWIN PRESS**
Classroom

*For information:*

Corwin Press
A SAGE Company
2455 Teller Road
Thousand Oaks, California 91320
CorwinPress.com

SAGE, Ltd.
1 Oliver's Yard
55 City Road
London EC1Y 1SP
United Kingdom

SAGE India Pvt. Ltd.
B 1/I 1 Mohan Cooperative
Industrial Area
Mathura Road, New Delhi
India 110 044

SAGE Asia-Pacific Pvt. Ltd.
33 Pekin Street #02-01
Far East Square
Singapore 048763

ISBN: 978-1-4129-5829-5

This book is printed on acid-free paper.

08  09  10  11  12  10 9 8 7 6 5 4 3 2 1

Executive Editor: Kathleen Hex
Managing Developmental Editor: Christine Hood
Editorial Assistant: Anne O'Dell
Developmental Writers: Allyson Burnett and Raymond Lowery
Developmental Editor: Carolea Williams
Proofreader: Carrie Reiling
Art Director: Anthony D. Paular
Design Project Manager: Jeffrey Stith
Cover Designers: Michael Dubowe and Jeffrey Stith
Illustrator: Scott Rolfs
Design Consultant: The Development Source

GRADES **4–8**

## TABLE OF CONTENTS

# Introduction

The objective of reading instruction is not only to enable students to read fluently and independently, but most importantly, to read with comprehension. Comprehension is the ability to construct meaning from text. By understanding what they have read, students are better able to remember, communicate, and apply the information they have gained through reading.

Developing reading comprehension also improves cognitive skills. Good readers think about what they read, and they are continually engaged in an ongoing dialogue with the text. Over time, reading extends their thinking. The structure and logic of written language enables the learner to more easily compose and grasp complex thoughts and meanings.

This book addresses four essential cognitive strategies that proficient readers need in order to unlock the meaning of written material. These strategies include questioning, summarizing, organizing, and monitoring.

- The **questioning strategy** teaches students to be mind readers. It challenges them to ask questions about what they read and to interact with the text.

- The **summarizing strategy** helps students "get the gist" or main idea of the text. It challenges students to restate the meaning in their own words.

- The **monitoring strategy** gives students concrete ways to "fix up their mix-ups" by thinking about how and what they are reading *while* they are actually reading.

- The **organizing strategy** invites students to represent information from text in a graphic format in order to see the big picture.

Teaching cognitive strategies is vastly different from teaching "skills." Skills are procedures readers learn through repetition. Strategies tap higher-order thinking skills that will help students meet the demands of every unique reading task. Helping students develop these literacy strategies will enhance and enlarge the scope of their learning. Students will then be better equipped to become independent learners and readers within every content area.

Reading comprehension empowers students, giving them the ability to explore virtually any topic or subject in which they are interested. This book can help teachers instill the joy of reading, which, in turn, can lead to a lifetime of fulfillment and success.

978-1-4129-5829-5

# Put It Into Practice

An often repeated urban school myth states that many students are able to "word call" (i.e., nail the correct pronunciation of every word they encounter) but do not understand the meaning of what they read. Some say students are word callers because they had too much phonics instruction and too few opportunities to engage in meaningful literacy activities. This fallacy is often used to convince teachers not to waste time teaching decoding strategies when other compensating strategies (such as using context clues) will work just as well.

An in-depth study of 361 students in the early elementary grades examined various comprehension and decoding difficulties (Shankweiler et al., 1999). Students were tested on word and non-word reading, reading and listening comprehension, and language and cognitive ability. Those who did comparatively well at decoding, but whose comprehension was lower, were less common than students who were low in both decoding *and* comprehension. Low reading comprehension can occur in students with well-developed word-reading skills, but the most likely cause is ineffective instruction in vocabulary and reading comprehension strategies.

Cognitive strategies used to increase comprehension are an important piece of the Reading Puzzle. The Reading Puzzle is a way of organizing and understanding reading instruction, as introduced in my book, *Teach Them All to Read: Catching the Kids Who Fall Through the Cracks* (2002). The puzzle contains the essential reading skills that students need to master in order to become literate at every grade level. *The Reading Puzzle, Grades 4–8* series focuses on five of these skills: Spelling, Word Analysis, Fluency, Vocabulary, and Comprehension.

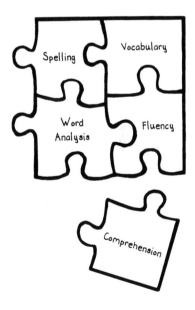

To describe what skilled readers do when they use cognitive strategies, I have coined the term *brain-based reading*. Brain-based reading is characterized by intentional action by the reader. It is the exact opposite of what some teachers call laughingly "brain-dead" reading, in which students simply stare at the page hoping for a cognitive miracle.

Cognitive strategies tap higher-order thinking skills in response to the demands of unique reading tasks. Strategies are used situationally. Students learn *how* and *when* to use cognitive strategies rather than "helping themselves" from a smorgasbord of content.

My vision for model instruction includes an extensive strategic reading program using only four strategies with related permutations and combinations. These four cognitive strategies include: questioning, summarizing, organizing, and monitoring.

978-1-4129-5829-5

Students at every grade level must be shown how to use cognitive strategies through modeling; coached to proficiency through guided practice; and then expected to routinely explain, elaborate, or defend their positions or answers before, during, and after reading. When students are expected from the earliest grades to articulate explanations, they become accustomed to evaluating, integrating, and elaborating knowledge in new ways.

## Questioning

Students should be the ones both asking the questions and then answering them, as well as replying to their classmates' questions. "Mind-reading" is a savvy questioning strategy. It looks something like this: Identify the most important ideas or concepts; process and manipulate the ideas into personal schema by using graphic organizers and summarizing the material; then pose questions to which one already has the answers. This kind of processing (rehearsal, review, comparing, contrasting, and making connections) increases the likelihood that students' newly acquired knowledge will be stored in long-term memory.

## Summarizing

Summarizing can be described as getting the gist of what is read. Most students have difficulty summarizing what they have read. That is, unless they have seen the summarizing strategy modeled numerous times, been carefully taught the various aspects of the strategy, and then had the opportunity to practice in cooperative groups with teacher supervision—all before being expected to summarize on their own (Brown & Day, 1983; Brown, Day, & Jones, 1983).

## Organizing

Organizing involves constructing graphic or visual representations that "help the learner to comprehend, summarize, and synthesize complex ideas in ways that, in many instances, surpass verbal statements" (Jones, Pierce, & Hunter, 1988/1989). By the time students enter high school, they should be able to construct various graphic organizers to help them understand what they read and organize their thoughts before writing (e.g., flowcharts, Venn diagrams, word webs, and so on).

## Monitoring

Monitoring involves two related and often seemingly simultaneous abilities: thinking about how and what one is reading for the purposes of determining if one is comprehending the text, and using various strategies to aid in comprehension. Monitoring begins before the reader actually reads any text and continues long after the reader has finished reading.

# CHAPTER 1

# Questioning Strategy

Asking questions is a big part of what teachers typically do. However, *students* should be the ones asking the questions. Questioning is a way that skilled readers:

- Interact with the text or the author to construct meaning

- Predict what is most important in the text

- Engage in dialogues with peers and teachers

To develop this essential strategy, give students opportunities to develop their own questions rather than act as passive respondents to teacher-developed questions. When students hear classmates or the teacher give correct answers to questions, they often have no clue why the answer is an appropriate one. It is when students actually both generate and answer higher-level questions that they become strategic questioners and readers.

The questioning strategy is multifaceted and can be used in tandem with other essential strategies. Students can use the questioning strategy to:

- Ask the author (in a figurative sense)

- Quiz themselves to make sure they are understanding main ideas

- Generate questions to ask classmates

- Figure out which questions their teacher might ask them

- Ask the teacher about something that is confusing or unknown

Teaching students how to use the questioning strategy in all of its combinations and permutations goes far beyond just asking higher-level questions after students have read a text selection. When students are able to generate their own questions, they will begin to determine the extent of their own learning.

BE A
MIND
READER

# What Will Happen Next?

While reading, skilled readers train their minds to predict what they think will happen next. To do this, they are always asking questions about the information they are gathering. In this activity, students will predict what is likely to happen next using information they gather while reading.

1. Explain that predictions are based on observation, experience, and reasoning. Read the following scenarios aloud to students. Challenge students to make predictions about what they think will happen next.

   - Elijah got a part-time job after school to earn some extra money. He was hoping to buy a new skateboard. He got his first paycheck on Friday.
   - Maria and her mother drove to the computer store. Maria had the money she received from her grandmother for her birthday.
   - The storm began suddenly and continued to grow more intense. Lightning flashed in the sky and thunder boomed loudly. The electricity blinked on and off.

2. Give each student a copy of the **What Will Happen Next? reproducible (page 9)**. Have students read each scenario and then write their predictions about the events they think will happen next.

3. Have students use the checklist at the bottom of the reproducible to evaluate their predictions. Encourage them to revise their predictions if needed.

4. Have students share and compare their predictions in small groups.

978-1-4129-5829-5

# What Will Happen Next?

**Directions:** Read each scenario. Based on the clues, predict what you think will happen next. Use the Prediction Checklist to guide your predictions. Check off the predictions if you can answer *yes* to each question in the checklist. If you cannot, revise your predictions.

| Here's What You Know . . . | What Will Happen Next? | Check |
|---|---|---|
| Crystal usually takes her dog for a walk after dinner. It was storming outside when Crystal finished dinner. | | |
| DeMarcus usually puts his homework in his backpack at the end of the day. When he gets home, he works on it before going outside to hang out with his friends. DeMarcus has just gotten home from school. | | |
| Phillip borrowed his older brother's MP3 player and accidentally lost it. Phillip told his mother what happened. | | |
| By Monday afternoon, Roberto had spent a week's worth of lunch money on a CD. His mother had warned him about using his money wisely. Roberto's mother found the new CD lying on his desk. | | |
| Hilda is waiting until Sunday to begin reading a 300-page book. The book report is due Monday morning. | | |

**Prediction Checklist**
- Is your prediction closely connected to what has already happened?
- Can you explain the reasons for your prediction?
- Does your prediction make sense and seem reasonable?

# Making Inferences

To successfully implement the questioning strategy, students must be able to ask questions whose answers can only be determined with inferential reasoning. In this activity, students become familiar with inferential reasoning by answering questions that require them to "read between the lines."

1. Tell students that to make an inference, they must be good detectives and notice every clue and detail the author provides. Then they must put this information together with what they already know.

2. Make a transparency of the **Catch a Clue: Set 1 reproducible (page 11)**. Reveal only the first statement: *The rider hung on tightly with both legs to avoid being tossed to the ground.*

3. Invite students to think aloud as they volunteer thoughts about where this event is happening based on the clues.

4. Give each student a copy of the Catch a Clue: Set 1 reproducible. Invite students to read the statements in the left column. They will answer the questions based on their ability to make inferences from the text. Have students write their responses in the boxes.

5. After students have completed the exercise, have them share their answers in pairs, groups, or with the entire class. Invite students to explain how they arrived at their inferences.

6. Repeat the activity on another day using the **Catch a Clue: Set 2** and **Catch a Clue: Set 3 reproducibles (pages 12–13)**.

# Catch a Clue: Set 1

**Directions:** Read each statement on the left. Gather clues and use what you know to answer the questions.

| Location or Setting | Where is this happening? |
|---|---|
| The rider hung on tightly with both legs to avoid being tossed to the ground. | |
| The girl felt the tide sweep her further away until she could no longer see the umbrellas. | |
| **Career or Occupation** | **What is this person's occupation?** |
| She swirled the frosting around the cake and then placed it in the display case. | |
| He went through his checklist and then got permission from the tower before take-off. | |
| **Instrument or Tool** | **What is the tool?** |
| She said, "You have a very high fever." | |
| Long before he made his first cut, the lumberjack knew which way the oak would fall. | |
| **Object** | **What is the object?** |
| There was something in the display window to please every shopper—beanbags, wingbacks, and even rockers. | |
| Maya wanted one that was self-cleaning and big enough to cook a 20-pound turkey. | |

# Catch a Clue: Set 2

**Directions:** Read each statement on the left. Gather clues and use what you know to answer the questions.

| Action | What is the action? |
|---|---|
| She ran the bases in record time but was called out at home plate. | |
| He saw the ripple in the water and cast his fly in the stream where he hoped it would be eaten. | |
| **Time** | **What is the time?** |
| The birds were singing, and the sun was high in the sky. | |
| The leaves in the trees were mostly orange and brown. | |
| **Feelings** | **What is the feeling?** |
| I won first prize in the science fair. | |
| No one was home except me, but I thought I heard footsteps in the living room. | |
| **Category** | **What is the category?** |
| We have been to Disneyland and Sea World, and we are going to Legoland next. | |
| I did not know that white-tipped, tiger, bull, and great whites were all in the same family. | |

# Catch a Clue: Set 3

**Directions:** Read each statement on the left. Gather clues and use what you know to answer the questions.

| Cause | What is the cause? |
|---|---|
| My room has never looked so neat. | |
| My book report was not completed on time. | |
| **Effect** | **What is the effect?** |
| I rode the Ferris wheel three times. | |
| I ate a whole cake all by myself. | |
| **Problem** | **What is the problem?** |
| I have to stop eating so many ice-cream sandwiches. | |
| I need to watch how loud I play my music. | |
| **Solution** | **What is the solution?** |
| I need money to buy a birthday present for my mom. | |
| I have 30 math problems to complete by Friday. | |

# Be a Mind Reader

Setting a purpose for reading is an effective comprehension strategy. In this activity, students will predict possible causes of an event or situation before reading about it. Their purpose for reading is to verify their predictions.

1. Ask students: *What do you think causes earthquakes?* Challenge them to be "mind readers" by brainstorming possible causes an author might describe in an article about earthquakes. Record their ideas on chart paper. Review all of the ideas and ask students to help you choose and underline the three most probable causes from the list.

2. Make a transparency of the **What Causes Earthquakes? reproducible (page 15)** and distribute copies to students. Read the article together as a class. Invite students to look for causes that are mentioned in the article.

3. After reading the selection, ask students to determine if their most probable causes were accurate. Ask if they were, therefore, able to read the author's mind before reading the article.

4. After modeling the activity, give students a copy of the **What Do You Think? reproducible (page 16)**. Provide a text selection that involves cause and effect. Have students complete the question at the top of the page using information you provide. Then ask them to write probable causes that answer the prompt before reading the assigned text. Finally, have them read the text to verify their "mind-reading" abilities.

5. Use the same strategy for a text selection that presents a problem and a solution. Give students a copy of the **Be a Problem Solver reproducible (page 17)** to complete before reading the assigned text.

Name _____ Date _____

# What Causes Earthquakes?

Did you know that an earthquake is the result of the earth relieving a little stress? You might ride a bike or read a book to relieve stress, but the earth relieves pressure by "shifting around."

The shaking ground during an earthquake is the result of an abrupt shift of rock along a fracture in the earth. This fracture is called a *fault*. Scientists believe that earthquakes occur when slow movements inside the earth push against the earth's outer layer. This movement causes rocks to suddenly break and fragment into pieces called *plates*. Most earthquakes happen at the boundaries of these plates. This theory is called *plate tectonics*.

People have known about earthquakes for thousands of years, but they did not know what caused them. It was Bunjiro Koto, a geologist from Japan, who first suggested that earthquakes were caused by faults.

The next time you need to relieve a little stress, remember that the earth needs to relieve stress, too. You may pick up a good book, but the earth needs to shake! Plate tectonics theory helps explain how the earth "shakes off" stress.

# What Do You Think?

**Directions:** Brainstorm a list of possible causes. Draw a star beside the causes you think are most likely. Then read the assigned text. Draw a checkmark beside each cause you found in the text.

**What do you think causes** _____?

| ✓ | ★ | Possible Causes |
|---|---|---|
|   |   | 1. |
|   |   | 2. |
|   |   | 3. |
|   |   | 4. |
|   |   | 5. |
|   |   | 6. |

**Were you a good mind reader?**

Name _____ Date _____

# Be a Problem Solver

**Directions:** Brainstorm a list of possible solutions. Draw a star beside the solutions you think are most likely. Then read the assigned text. Draw a checkmark beside each solution you found in the text.

**What are some possible solutions for** _____?

| ✓ | ★ | Possible Solutions |
|---|---|---|
|   |   | 1. |
|   |   | 2. |
|   |   | 3. |
|   |   | 4. |
|   |   | 5. |
|   |   | 6. |

**Were you a good mind reader?**

# Questioning with Fascinating Facts

When students begin questioning what the text is about before actually reading it, they begin the "mind-reading" process, a key strategy for improving comprehension. In this activity, students anticipate what a reading assignment is about based on a given fascinating fact.

1. Select a passage for students to read. As you preview the text, search for an interesting fact or detail. Use this fact to capture students' attention and generate interest around what students will be reading.

2. To model this activity for students, read aloud this fascinating fact: *Although cows graze up to eight hours a day, taking in about 100 pounds of feed and about a bathtub full of water, they have no upper front teeth.*

3. Make a transparency of the **I Wonder . . . reproducible (page 19)**. Using the transparency template, ask students to create "I wonder" statements based on the fascinating fact. Write students' ideas on the transparency. While student responses will vary, they might wonder:

> **How** a cow chews its food
>
> **What** a cow likes to eat
>
> **When** a cow sleeps
>
> **Where** a cow finds its food
>
> **Why** a cow has no upper front teeth
>
> **What would happen if** a cow did have front teeth
>
> **What else** is unusual about a cow

4. After students understand how to use a fascinating fact to generate "I wonder" statements, give each student a copy of the I Wonder . . . reproducible.

5. Write a fascinating fact on the board that you have chosen from a text selection. Have students copy it onto their reproducible. Then invite them to generate their own "I wonder" statements related to the fascinating fact.

6. Invite students to read the assigned text. Then have them complete the reproducible by recording information they discovered that answers their questions.

978-1-4129-5829-5

# I Wonder . . .

**Directions:** Write the fascinating fact in the box. Complete the sentences in the left column with "I wonder" statements related to the fact. Then read the assigned text. Write what you found out in the right column.

**Fascinating Fact**

| I Wonder . . . | I Found Out |
|---|---|
| How | |
| What | |
| When | |
| Where | |
| Why | |
| What would happen if | |
| What else | |

## Questioning Quadrant

The "mind-reading" strategy might involve students predicting the questions that you will ask on a quiz. It might also involve understanding what questions the author was answering when writing the text. In this activity, students will learn the four types of questions they must be able to ask.

1. Draw the **Questioning Quadrant (page 23)** on chart paper. Explain to students that each quadrant corresponds to a different type of information and therefore, a different type of question.

   **Quad A: In the Text (Right There)** is for information found in one specific place in the text.

   **Quad B: In the Text (Pull It Together)** is for information found by pulling together ideas from several places in the text.

   **Quad C: In Your Head (Use Inference)** is for information found by "reading between the lines" or making inferences.

   **Quad D: In Your Head (Use Your Own Experience)** is for information related to the text that can only be discovered from the reader's own experience.

2. Give students a copy of the **Are You Ready for a Puppy? reproducible (page 22)**. Display a transparency of the reproducible on the overhead projector as you read aloud the text for students. Invite them to follow along. Read two or three sentences at a time and stop to think aloud in response to what you have read.

3. Write one or two questions in each quadrant on the chart paper. For example, based on the text selection "Are You Ready for a Puppy?," you might formulate these questions:

**Quad A: In the Text (Right There)**
- *What are some activities dogs enjoy?*

**Quad B: In the Text (Pull It Together)**
- *What types of things should you consider before getting a puppy?*
- *What are some benefits of owning a puppy?*

**Quad C: In Your Head (Use Inference)**
- *What type of person would make the best dog owner?*
- *How would being a dog owner change your life?*

**Quad D: In Your Head (Use Your Own Experience)**
- *What is the first thing you would do if you got a new puppy?*
- *Do you agree or disagree with this statement? "There is nothing better than finding a four-legged, tail-wagging friend waiting for you when you come home from school."*
- *In what ways is being a dog owner related to being a parent?*

4. After modeling this strategy for students, repeat the activity on another day using a new text selection. Invite the class to think aloud about the text and contribute questions to the quadrant.

5. On another day, have students complete the process independently. This three-step process—*I do it. We do it. You do it.*—may take several weeks of instruction and practice.

# Are You Ready for a Puppy?

Of course, you can't wait for that cute little ball of fur to turn your new sneakers into expensive doggy toys. You can't wait to slip that leash over your puppy's head and stroll through the park as your puppy forges ahead and pulls you along. Let's be honest, there is nothing better than finding a four-legged, tail-wagging friend waiting for you when you come home from school. Dogs are lovable, energetic, affectionate, and fun. They make wonderful companions. They love to play, go for walks, and have all kinds of mischievous fun.

But dogs, like all pets, are a tremendous amount of responsibility. Dogs are great companions to take hiking or to the beach, to cuddle with in front of the television, and so much more. However, dogs also require a lot of attention and care. They require care even on days when you might rather just play a video game or go to the movies with your friends. Just a few things included in everyday dog care are feeding, grooming, walking, playing, and of course, lots of love.

Be sure to ask yourself some important questions before adding that cute, furry companion to your life. Are you willing to spend the time necessary to properly care for a dog? Does your home have a yard? Will you be able to walk your dog daily? Do you have the resources to make regular visits to a veterinarian? Do you want an active dog or a laid-back dog? Do you want a big dog or a small dog? Be responsible and take time to think about your decision. Then you can truly enjoy the happiness that being a dog owner can bring.

# Questioning Quadrant

**Directions:** Read the assigned text. Read two or three sentences at a time and stop to think about what you are reading. Write at least two questions in each quadrant.

| **Quad A: In the Text (Right There)** | **Quad B: In the Text (Pull It Together)** |
|---|---|
| | |
| **Quad C: In Your Head (Use Inference)** | **Quad D: In Your Head (Use Your Own Experience)** |
| | |

# Story Quadrant

After students read a story, they can build critical thinking skills by analyzing, applying, and evaluating what they have read. In this activity, students will gather information in four categories and then create questions using the information.

1. Draw a story quadrant on chart paper similar to that shown on the **Story Quadrant reproducible (page 25)**. Explain to students that each quadrant represents a different element found in a story—setting, plot, dialogue, and characters.

2. Read a short story aloud to students. Model how to think aloud about what you are reading as you read. As you run across text that describes or alludes to each story element, write the information on the chart. For example:

   **Setting:** one dreary cold morning, in the backyard

   **Plot:** find a treasure map in an old trunk, want to look for buried treasure

   **Dialogue:** talk about where to look and where to dig holes, decide on a plan

   **Characters:** Stella, ten-year-old girl, very adventurous, funny; Tanner, eleven-year-old boy, next-door neighbor, shy, intelligent

3. Make a transparency of the **Question Prompts reproducible (page 26)**. Show students how to apply the information you gathered in the Story Quadrant to the prompts. Write several sample questions to model for students.

4. After modeling this activity, give each pair of students a copy of the Story Quadrant and Question Prompts reproducibles. Invite students to gather information as they read an assigned story and then develop questions using the information.

5. After students have written their questions, invite them to share their writing with the class. Encourage volunteers to answer the questions.

Name _____     Date _____

# Story Quadrant

**Directions:** Read the story. While reading, write information about each topic in the boxes.

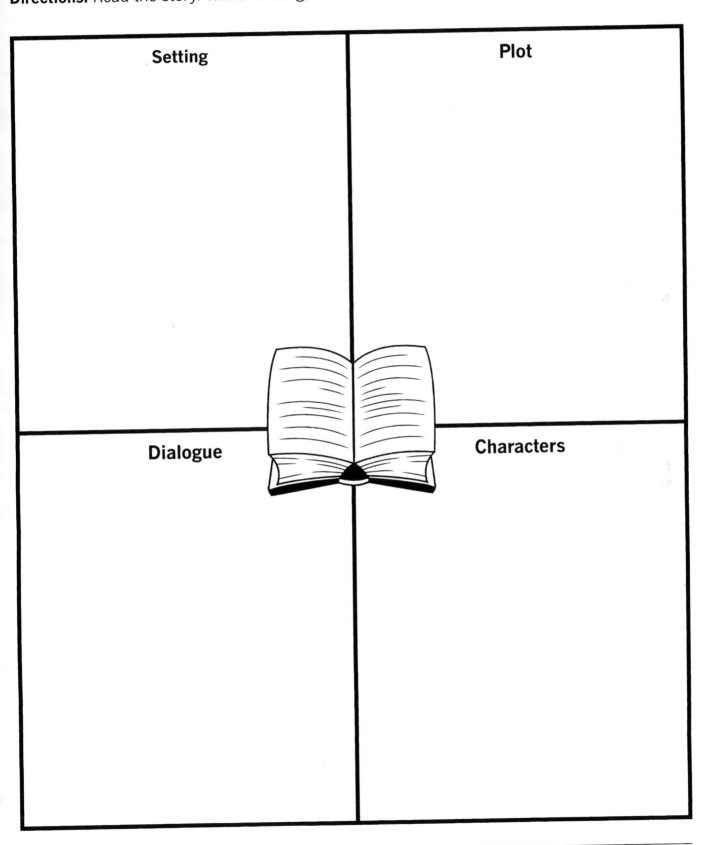

|  |  |
|---|---|
| **Setting** | **Plot** |
| **Dialogue** | **Characters** |

Name _____  Date _____

# Question Prompts

**Directions:** Use information from the Story Quadrant to write questions about your story. Use these prompts to help you.

1. What happened at _____?

2. What happened before/after _____?

3. Can you explain why _____?

4. How did what _____ said affect _____?

5. Who was it that _____?

6. What are the differences between _____ and _____?

7. Can you describe an example of _____?

8. What are some other solutions for _____?

9. What are some of _____'s problems?

10. Do you think _____ is a good or a bad thing? Why?

11. What would have happened if _____?

12. What questions would you ask of _____?

13. Where/What/Why/How/When did the main character _____?

14. If _____ had happened, what might the ending have been?

15. What was the theme of _____?

16. What is the meaning of _____?

17. Why did _____ act that way?

18. Can you list all the _____?

19. Can you relate to what happened when _____? Explain how.

20. How would you defend what _____ did?

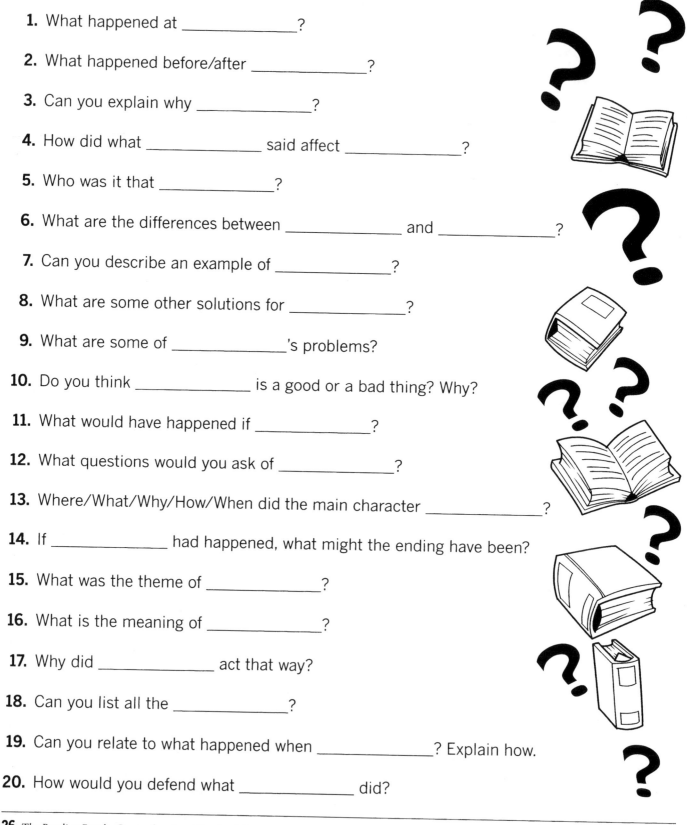

*Reproducible*  978-1-4129-5829-5 • © Corwin Press

# Change It Up

Predicting is a powerful "mind-reading" strategy. By guessing what might happen next, students become actively involved in the text they are reading. In this activity, students will predict how a situation might change if one of the variables in a story was altered.

1. Ask students if they have ever wished they could change the choices that characters or people make or the way a story or situation ends. Tell them that they will now have that opportunity.

2. After students have read the same story or assigned text, give them a copy of the **Change It Up reproducible (page 28)**. Ask students to complete the prompt: *What do you think would happen if _____?* by suggesting changes to the story. Remind them to think carefully about the different outcomes to the story were these changes actually to take place. Have students write their four story change ideas on their reproducible.

3. After students have brainstormed several ideas that would make interesting changes to the story, invite them to select one. Have students write a paragraph that answers the prompt with the idea they selected. For example: *What do you think would happen if Mark decided not to tell Elisha the secret?* or *What do you think would happen if the setting was at the circus instead of the shopping mall?*

4. Encourage volunteers to read their paragraphs aloud to the class, or post them on a bulletin board for others to read.

# Change It Up

**Directions:** Have you ever wished that you could change the choices that a character makes or the way a story ends? Now you can! Read the question prompt and answer it by suggesting some story changes.

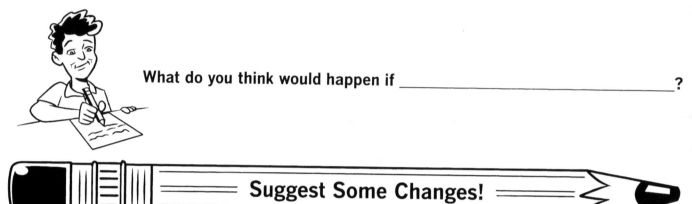

**What do you think would happen if** _____?

**Suggest Some Changes!**

| | |
|---|---|
| **1.** | |
| **2.** | |
| **3.** | |
| **4.** | |

**Directions:** Choose one of your changes. Then write a paragraph that answers the question.

**What do you think would happen if . . .**

_____

_____

_____

_____

_____

_____

_____

# Questioning to Compare

Considering how one idea or topic is similar to another is a questioning strategy that improves comprehension. In this activity, students will compare and identify similarities between two ideas or topics from a reading selection.

1. To model this activity, write the words *skateboard* and *rollerblades* on the board. Ask students: *How are skateboards and rollerblades alike?* Invite students to name characteristics that these two objects have in common. Students might respond that both have wheels, both are faster than walking, and both are fun to do with friends. Record their ideas on the board.

2. Give students a copy of the **Questioning to Compare reproducible (page 30)**. Assign students a text selection to read. You may choose to assign the two ideas or topics you want students to compare, or invite them to choose their own. If students are choosing what to compare, remind them that they can select two characters, ideas, objects, or events.

3. Discuss the lists students created as a prewriting activity. Ask students to write a paragraph about the similarities they found.

# Making Connections

Connecting new information with existing knowledge is a powerful strategy for improving comprehension and increasing long-term memory of new learning. In this activity, students will consider how new information is related to concepts with which they are already familiar.

1. This activity is especially helpful when you are teaching multiple related content lessons over the course of several days. Invite students to tie in learning from previous lessons to the new material.

2. Give each pair of students a copy of the **Making Connections reproducible (page 31)**. Choose a topic with which you want students to make a connection, and write it on the board. Ask students to use the topic to complete the sentence frame: *How does _____ connect with what we learned before?*

3. Have students read the assigned text to find ways the new learning relates to previous concepts. Then ask them to record their ideas on the reproducible by connecting two concepts in each pair of links.

978-1-4129-5829-5

# Questioning to Compare

**Directions:** After reading the assigned text, complete the question below. Then complete the chart by writing what the two items have in common.

**How are** _____ **and** _____ **alike?**

| They both . . . |
|---|
| 1. |
| 2. |
| 3. |
| 4. |
| 5. |

**Directions:** Write a paragraph using the list you created about how the two items are alike.

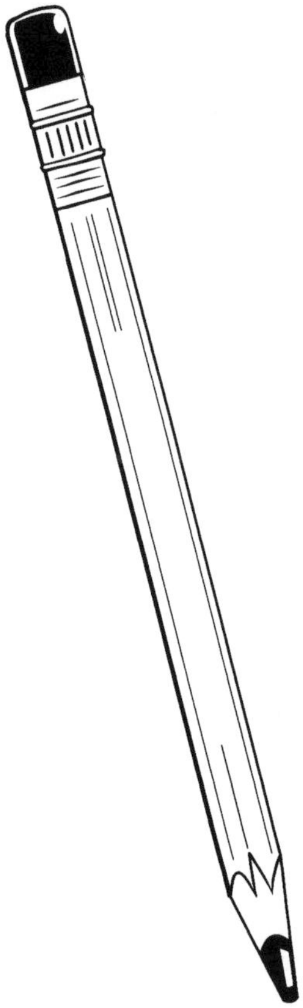

_____

_____

_____

_____

_____

_____

_____

_____

_____

_____

_____

_____

# Making Connections

**Directions:** Complete the question with a topic your teacher provides. Read the assigned text. Find ways that the new ideas connect with concepts you have learned before. Write connecting ideas in each pair of chain links.

How does _____ connect with what I learned before?

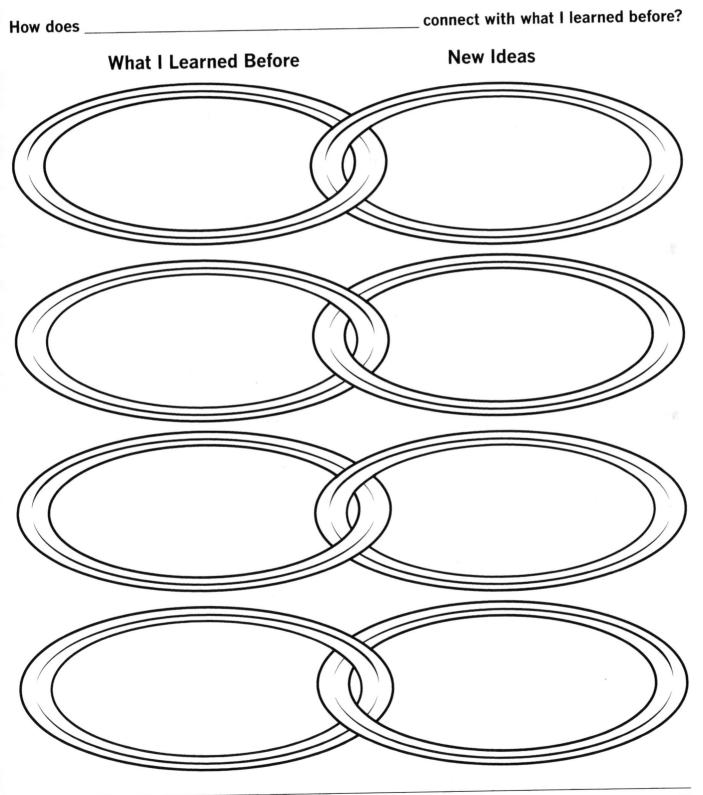

**What I Learned Before**          **New Ideas**

# CHAPTER 2

# Summarizing Strategy

Summarizing is the ability to "get the gist" or figure out the main idea of a passage. It is the ability to restate the meaning of what has been read in your own words. Summarizing is essential for helping students:

- Determine what is most important to remember about a paragraph or chapter

- Take notes for report writing

- Study prior to a test

- Read confusing text to find the kernels of important information

One of the hardest assignments for students is summarizing what they have read. To develop this strategy, students must see it modeled numerous times, both orally and in writing. Some activities that help students learn this valuable strategy include:

- Skimming through text to highlight, underline, or make notes about main ideas

- Dividing text into chunks to highlight main points and sub-points

- Identifying and deleting trivial and redundant information

- Skipping information that is difficult to understand and coming back to it later

- Collapsing lists by choosing key words

- Highlighting key ideas and writing a summary word or phrase for each

The summarization strategy is multifaceted and can be used in tandem with other essential strategies. Emphasize to students the benefits of "getting the gist," such as achieving better grades, scoring higher on tests, and being able to do research and take notes to make writing reports easier.

## GET THE GIST

# Putting the Pieces Together

Understanding the main idea is an essential component of reading comprehension. In this activity, students will find the main idea by highlighting key details for each chunk of text and then write a summary statement.

1. Review a text selection that you will assign students to read. Divide it into three chunks that represent the beginning, the middle, and the end.

2. Give each student a copy of the **Putting the Pieces Together reproducible (page 34)**. Help students identify the three predetermined sections of the text they will be reading.

3. Explain to students that understanding key points and concepts within the text are like finding separate puzzle pieces. When put together, these puzzle pieces form the "big picture." Invite students to find a "puzzle piece" within each text section as they read.

4. When students have finished reading the entire passage, have them "put the pieces together" to complete the prompt: *What is the main idea?*

# Getting the Gist

Summarizing is the ability to "get the gist" or figure out the main idea. This strategy is essential to determining what should be remembered about a paragraph or chapter. In this activity, students will practice their summarizing skills to get the gist of the main idea.

1. Remind students that getting the gist of a passage means understanding the main idea. Make a transparency of the **Getting the Gist reproducible (page 35)** and distribute a copy to each student. Read the first paragraph aloud for students. Think aloud as you demonstrate how to summarize what the paragraph is about.

2. After modeling the activity, invite students to work independently to complete the reproducible.

3. When students are done, invite volunteers to share their answers. Record summary statements on the transparency. Discuss variations and ask students to explain their thinking.

978-1-4129-5829-5

# Putting the Pieces Together

**Directions:** Identify the beginning, middle, and end sections of the assigned text. As you finish reading each section, write a summarizing sentence in each puzzle piece. After you finish the passage, write the main idea below.

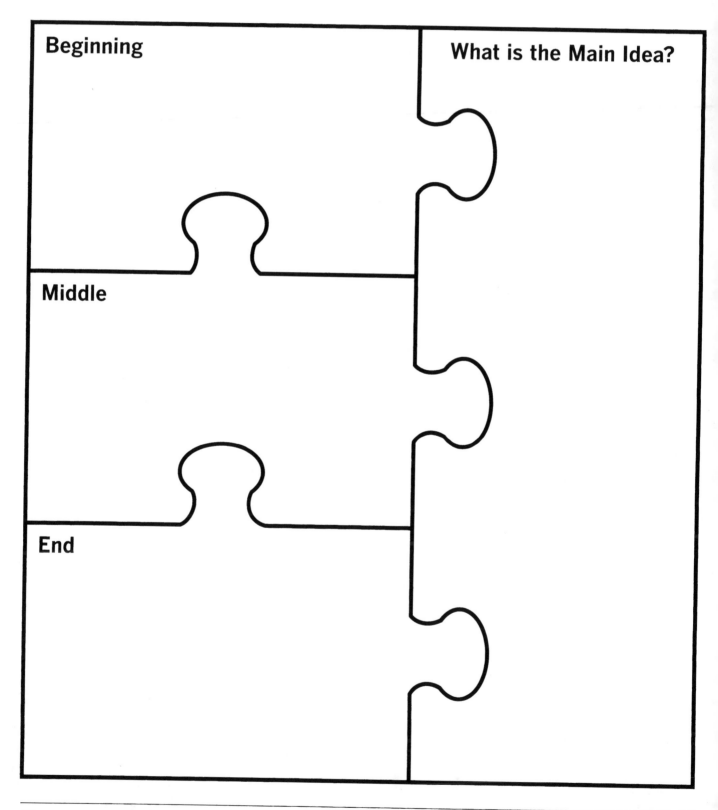

**Beginning**

**What is the Main Idea?**

**Middle**

**End**

# Getting the Gist

**Directions:** Read each paragraph. Then write a statement to show that you "get the gist" of what the paragraph is mainly about.

The storm arrived at midnight. It woke up everyone in the house with loud crashes of thunder and driving rain that beat on the roof and windows. The dog hid under the bed. The children ran to their parents' room. Flashlights in hand, the parents grabbed some candles and a radio in preparation for a long night with no sleep.

_____

The rodeo came to town each year. The town hosted a parade, and the children wore their Western clothes to school. Everyone talked about which performer they wanted to see at the rodeo.

_____

Casey's favorite movie was *Cinderella*. She loved the songs, the dancing, and the beautiful dresses at the dance. Even though Casey knew that Cinderella would end up marrying the prince, she always felt sad when Cinderella ran away from the dance, leaving her glass slipper behind.

_____

The first day of school is both exciting and confusing. It's exciting to see friends you haven't seen in months and catch up on what happened over the summer. However, it can be confusing to get used to a new schedule and new teachers.

_____

As always, March brought gusty winds. This was Austin's favorite time of year because he was an expert kite flyer. Today was warm and sunny, and the wind was just right. Austin couldn't wait to get his new kite in the air, so he could watch it dance in the bright blue sky.

_____

# Give It a Name

Research has shown that summarization instruction improves students' recall of what they read. In this activity, students will read a short, descriptive paragraph and summarize their thoughts using one word.

1. Make a transparency of the **Give It a Name reproducible (page 37)** and place it on the overhead projector. Reveal to students the paragraph in the first box and read it together as a class. Invite students to brainstorm words that best describe the main idea of the text. Write the words on the board. Then ask students to identify the one word they think best describes the paragraph. Circle that word on the board and then write it in the first pencil on the transparency.

2. Give students a copy of both **Give It a Name reproducibles (pages 37–38)**. Invite them to read each paragraph and write one word that summarizes the gist of the text. While answers will vary, here are some possible words students might use:
   1. ill-mannered, slob
   2. messy, unorganized
   3. helpful, polite, giving
   4. dangerous, hazardous
   5. strict, insensitive
   6. lonely, solitary, isolated
   7. exciting, fun
   8. snob, conceited
   9. negotiate, bargain, inexpensive
   10. smart, popular, successful
   11. gentle, shy, hesitant
   12. beautiful, breathtaking

3. After students have completed the reproducibles, invite them to share and explain their answers. List students' words on the board, and ask the class to vote on the most specific, descriptive word for each paragraph.

978-1-4129-5829-5

# Give It a Name

**Directions:** Read each paragraph. Write one word inside each pencil that best describes the "gist" of that paragraph. Be prepared to explain why you chose each word.

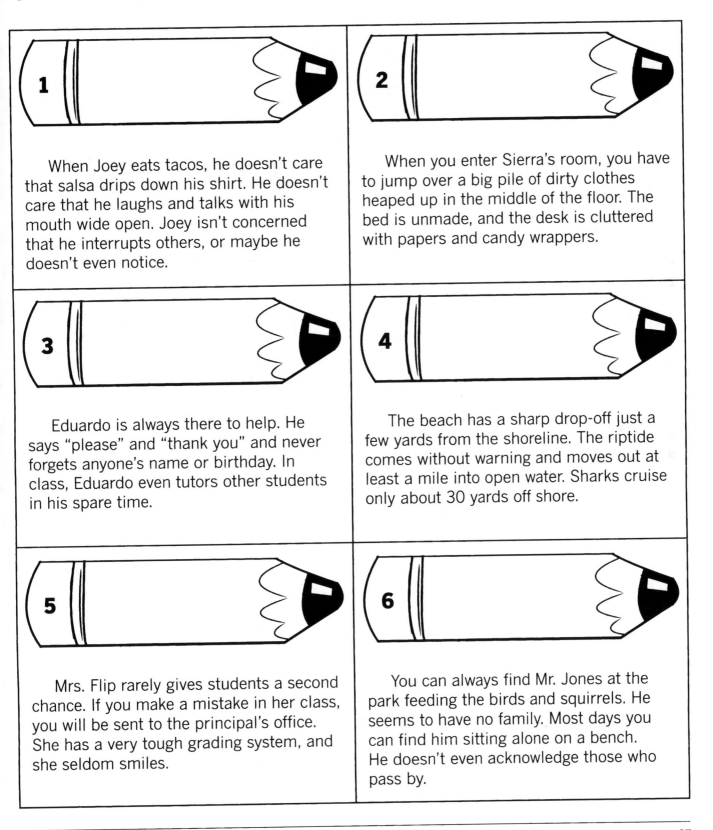

**1**

When Joey eats tacos, he doesn't care that salsa drips down his shirt. He doesn't care that he laughs and talks with his mouth wide open. Joey isn't concerned that he interrupts others, or maybe he doesn't even notice.

**2**

When you enter Sierra's room, you have to jump over a big pile of dirty clothes heaped up in the middle of the floor. The bed is unmade, and the desk is cluttered with papers and candy wrappers.

**3**

Eduardo is always there to help. He says "please" and "thank you" and never forgets anyone's name or birthday. In class, Eduardo even tutors other students in his spare time.

**4**

The beach has a sharp drop-off just a few yards from the shoreline. The riptide comes without warning and moves out at least a mile into open water. Sharks cruise only about 30 yards off shore.

**5**

Mrs. Flip rarely gives students a second chance. If you make a mistake in her class, you will be sent to the principal's office. She has a very tough grading system, and she seldom smiles.

**6**

You can always find Mr. Jones at the park feeding the birds and squirrels. He seems to have no family. Most days you can find him sitting alone on a bench. He doesn't even acknowledge those who pass by.

# Give It a Name

**Directions:** Read each paragraph. Write one word inside each pencil that best describes the "gist" of that paragraph. Be prepared to explain why you chose each word.

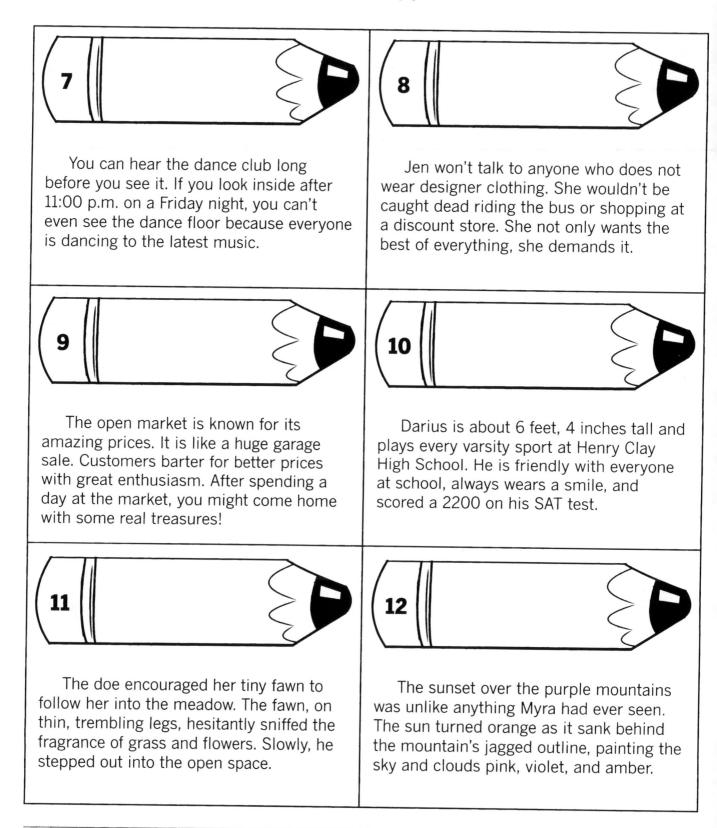

**7**

You can hear the dance club long before you see it. If you look inside after 11:00 p.m. on a Friday night, you can't even see the dance floor because everyone is dancing to the latest music.

**8**

Jen won't talk to anyone who does not wear designer clothing. She wouldn't be caught dead riding the bus or shopping at a discount store. She not only wants the best of everything, she demands it.

**9**

The open market is known for its amazing prices. It is like a huge garage sale. Customers barter for better prices with great enthusiasm. After spending a day at the market, you might come home with some real treasures!

**10**

Darius is about 6 feet, 4 inches tall and plays every varsity sport at Henry Clay High School. He is friendly with everyone at school, always wears a smile, and scored a 2200 on his SAT test.

**11**

The doe encouraged her tiny fawn to follow her into the meadow. The fawn, on thin, trembling legs, hesitantly sniffed the fragrance of grass and flowers. Slowly, he stepped out into the open space.

**12**

The sunset over the purple mountains was unlike anything Myra had ever seen. The sun turned orange as it sank behind the mountain's jagged outline, painting the sky and clouds pink, violet, and amber.

# Using Details to Summarize

As mentioned previously, summarizing is one of the most difficult comprehension strategies for students to master. Students must see summarization strategies modeled many times before they can be successful using these strategies independently. In this activity, students will practice chunking a text selection into categories, noting details about each category and then summarizing those details.

1. Display a transparency of the **In the Courtyard reproducible (page 40)** and distribute copies to students. Use this text passage to model the activity. Read the text aloud as students follow along.

2. After reading the text, create a three-column chart on the board. Title the columns *Location, People,* and *Activities.* Invite students to follow along again as you reread the text. This time, think aloud while reading to point out details related to each category.

3. Invite students to recall the details you identified. Write their ideas on the board in the appropriate columns.

4. When the chart is complete, ask a volunteer to read aloud all the details recorded for one category. Invite the class to brainstorm a one-sentence summary of those details. Repeat with the other two categories. When the activity is complete, the class will have written three sentences that represent a summary of the text.

5. Divide the class into cooperative groups of three or four. Give each group a copy of the **It's All in the Details reproducible (page 41)**. Assign each group a passage. They will read the passage, categorize the topics, record details, and then summarize each set of details in one sentence.

6. Invite groups to share their completed work with the class.

# In the Courtyard

The first buses begin dropping off students in the morning at about 6:30 a.m. By 7:00 a.m., all of the buses have dumped their weary occupants into the bus drive. Students arrive half asleep, carrying books and backpacks. Some are listening to music, with ear buds in their ears. Others are talking to friends on their cell phones. But everyone is headed toward the courtyard, which is in the center of the school.

Once most students have gone to their lockers, they begin to form into groups in the courtyard. Some students sit at the picnic tables that are permanently bolted in place to eat their breakfast. You can usually find the same people eating at the same tables day after day. The boys' soccer team and their girlfriends dominate two tables. The cheerleaders sit at another table. The chess club has laid claim to another table. On the small, grassy hill at the courtyard's north end, skateboarders, along with sprinklings of students who have spiked hair, rule. In front of this small hill, kids are playing a form of hacky sack, but they usually end up turning the game into dodge ball. On the various benches placed throughout the courtyard, groups of friends sit in clumps of threes and fours, talking, laughing, sharing secrets, and gossiping. Not all students are with someone—some are standing alone along one of the walls, usually listening to something on their MP3 players, looking bored or completely lost in the music.

Teachers and administrators patrol the courtyard, stopping now and then to talk to students and constantly reminding those who get too loud to settle down. When the first bell rings for first-period class, the students are slow to react and then begin to move reluctantly to their classrooms. By the third and final bell, all that remains in the courtyard are the wrappers from some students' snacks and the echo of administrators and hall monitors calling out to a few straggling students who, although they know they have nowhere else to go, still do not want to go to class.

# It's All in the Details

**Directions:** Read the assigned text selection. Then record details about the location, people, and actions you read about. When you have gathered all the details, write a one-sentence summary below each box.

**Location**

Summary: _____

**People**

Summary: _____

**Actions**

Summary: _____

# The Five W's

A news article is a great source for teaching students to summarize a main idea. In this activity, students will summarize the lead paragraph of a news article and then determine if the remainder of the article supports their summary.

1. Explain to students that the lead paragraph of a news article usually follows a predictable pattern. It contains the key elements that will be further discussed in the article (who, what, where, why, and when). Display a transparency of the **Surfing at the White House? reproducible (page 43)**, and show only the first paragraph of the article. Read aloud and identify the five W's in the lead paragraph.

   **Who:** Tim Turner

   **What:** Got a request to design a shirt

   **Where:** Seaside Surf Shop

   **Why:** For the President's birthday

   **When:** In less than two weeks

2. Based on the five W's, write a summary sentence that reflects the main idea. For example:

   *This article is mostly about a local surf shop employee, Tim Turner, having a special opportunity to design a shirt for the President of the United States.*

3. Then reveal the remainder of the article for students to read. Ask students if the summary statement was supported by the entire article. If not, ask them to help you revise the summary statement.

4. After modeling this activity, give students articles from a local newspaper and a copy of **The Five W's reproducible (page 44)**. You may also allow students to choose an article on their own. Have students use the news article to complete The Five W's reproducible. Invite them to work independently or in small groups.

978-1-4129-5829-5

# Surfing at the White House?

Tim Turner, an employee at Florida's famous Seaside Surf Shop, got an unusual request. He was asked to design a custom Hawaiian shirt in less than two weeks. He might have rejected the request if the recipient of the shirt wasn't the President of the United States.

A White House official contacted the surf clothing company asking that a shirt be specially designed for the President's birthday. The company asked Tim Turner to take on the task and to do it as quickly as possible.

The design that Tim created featured many of the President's favorite images, including the Presidential Seal. It was completed and shipped in just six days. Tim was honored to make this one-of-a-kind shirt for the President and commented that he never dreamed he would have the opportunity to be a part of such a special birthday surprise.

Name _____ Date _____

# The Five W's

**Directions:** Read only the first paragraph of a news article. Write the Five W's from the lead paragraph. Then write a summary statement telling what the article is mostly about.

**Directions:** Now read the rest of the article to see if you were right.

| Yes, I was right! | After reading the article, I think the article was really about . . . |
| --- | --- |
| **STOP** | _____ |
| You don't have to do anything else. | _____ |

# Picture It!

Using visual images can help students practice finding the main idea. In this activity, students will write summary sentences to describe the main idea of a picture.

1. Collect pictures from a wide variety of sources such as:
   - digital prints of students at work
   - students' photos from home
   - magazine images
   - Internet photos
   - pictures from books

2. Make a transparency of one of the pictures you have collected. Show students the picture and think aloud as you model how to tell what the picture is mainly about. Write your ideas beside the picture. For example, if you show a picture of a baseball team celebrating a victory, you might say: *This baseball team just won a big game, and the players are celebrating their victory.*

3. Give students a copy of the **Picture It! reproducible (page 46)**. Invite students to select three pictures and glue a picture inside each frame. Encourage students to write the "gist," or what the picture is mainly about, beside each image.

4. Invite students to share their work in small groups or with the whole class. Ask them to identify specific images or items in the pictures that helped them summarize the main idea.

5. Post student work on a classroom bulletin board.

# Picture It!

**Directions:** Glue a picture inside each frame. On the lines beside each picture, write what the picture is mainly about.

# Character Summary

As mentioned previously, developing summarizing skills can be challenging for many students. Creating a character summary guided by specific questions gives students a more focused method to practice this strategy. In this activity, students will focus on one story character and create a summary that describes that character.

1. To model this activity, use a character from a fictional story with which your students are familiar. You may choose to use Stuart from *Stuart Little*, Charlotte or Wilbur from *Charlotte's Web*, Ralph from *The Mouse and the Motorcycle*, Billy from *Where the Red Fern Grows*, Ponyboy from *The Outsiders*, or any character your students enjoy and have read about.

2. Ask students the following questions about the character and write their responses on the board.
   - *What does this character look like?*
   - *What does this character do?*
   - *What are this character's likes and dislikes?*
   - *What does the character think or feel?*

3. Using the list of character details students created, think aloud as you summarize the details to write a summary paragraph. Then use the paragraph to introduce the character to the class. For example:

   *In* Where the Red Fern Grows, *Billy Colman has a bad case of "puppy love." More than anything in the world, he wants coonhounds. Throughout the book, Billy shows himself to be determined and brave, with lots of grit.*

4. After modeling the activity, give students a copy of the **Character Snapshot** and **Character Introduction reproducibles (pages 48–49)**. Assign students a text passage to read, and then invite them to choose one character for which to complete their own character snapshot.

5. Ask students who summarized the same character to form groups. Encourage group members to compare and contrast their summary introductions.

# Character Snapshot

**Directions:** Read the assigned text. Choose your favorite character. As you reread the story, pick out details that describe your character. Write the details in the picture snapshots.

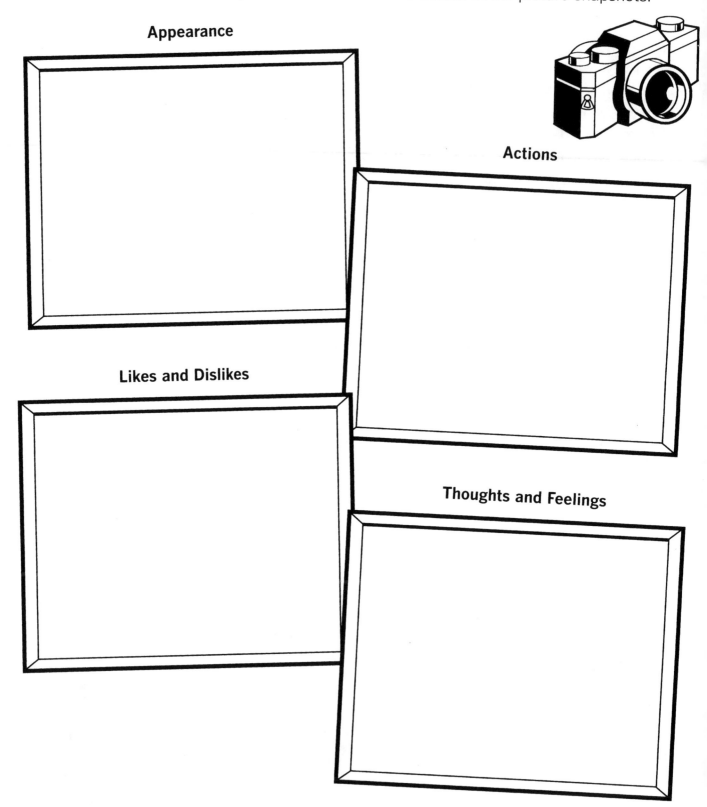

**Appearance**

**Actions**

**Likes and Dislikes**

**Thoughts and Feelings**

# Character Introduction

**Directions:** Now introduce your character to someone who has not read the story. Using details from the Character Snapshot sheet, write a short paragraph introducing the character.

<br>
<br>
<br>
<br>
<br>
<br>
<br>

**Directions:** Share and discuss your character introduction with a classmate who wrote about the same character. Did you both include the same details?

| Details in My Introduction | Details We Both Included | Details in My Partner's Introduction |
|---|---|---|
| | | |

## Headline Hints

Skimming through text to find details that support the main idea is one strategy readers might use to determine the gist of a passage. In this activity, students will search for details that support a headline.

1. After previewing a text selection you will assign students to read, create an interesting, attention-grabbing headline for it that reflects the main idea.

2. Give students a copy of the **Headline Hints reproducible (page 51)** and make a transparency of it. Write the headline you created on the transparency, and invite students to do the same on their copies.

3. Have students read the text passage in cooperative groups of three or four to find details that support the headline. Ask them to write the details inside the newspaper on their reproducible. Then have the group decide together on a summary sentence, based on the details, that describes the headline.

4. When groups have finished their work, ask them to share their ideas aloud. Record their ideas on the transparency. Encourage students to explain their thinking.

## Key Words and Phrases

Instead of summarizing text in their own words, students might copy from the author. Remind students that it is not proper to copy text word-for-word. Explain the meaning of the word *plagiarism* and the importance of summarizing in one's own words. This is called *paraphrasing*.

However, recording key words and phrases from a text is a helpful middle step between reading and writing a summary. Graphic organizers are useful tools that help students choose and record key words or phrases to sum up ideas from a paragraph or passage.

1. Be sure that students understand the idea of key words, phrases, and concepts prior to this activity. Review how to identify these items in a sample section of text. Then give students a copy of the **Summary Circle Organizer (page 52)**.

2. Assign students a chapter from a textbook. Ask them to write key words or phrases from each paragraph or section in one of the boxes surrounding the circle.

3. Once students read the entire chapter, have them summarize the details by writing two or three sentences in the center circle.

# Headline Hints

**Directions:** Write the given headline on the line. Then read the assigned text. Find and record details that support the headline.

**Headline**

1. _____

2. _____

3. _____

4. _____

5. _____

6. _____

7. _____

8. _____

**Directions:** Combine the details to write a one-sentence summary.

_____

_____

_____

# Summary Circle Organizer

**Directions:** Read the assigned text. Write key words and phrases for each paragraph or section in each box. When you finish reading, use your words and phrases to write a two- or three-sentence summary in the center circle.

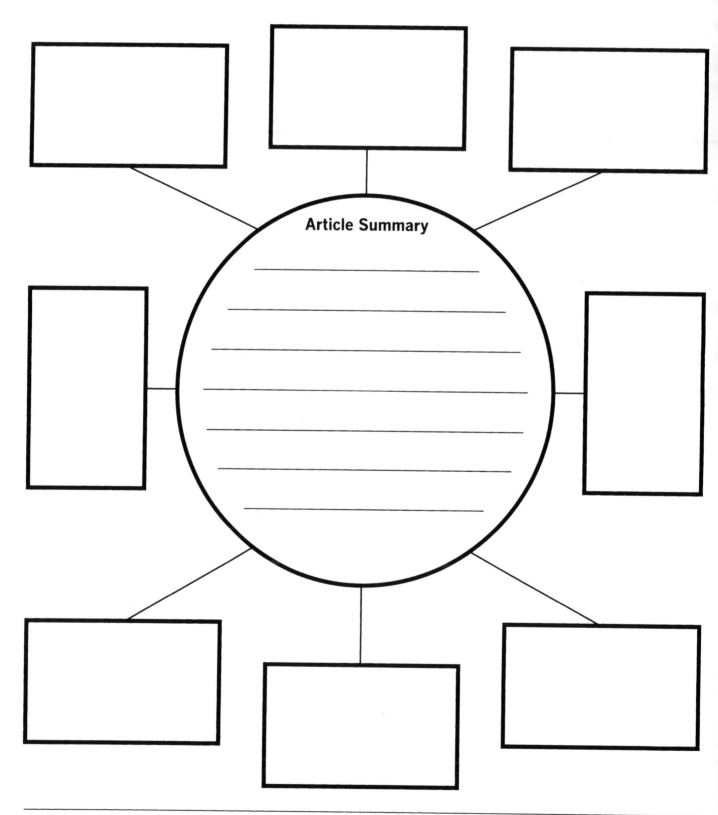

**Article Summary**

# News Story Summary

Give students many, varied opportunities to identify important details in text to hone their summarizing skills. In this activity, students must determine the missing headline for a news story by focusing on important details.

1. Make a transparency of the **One Last Ride reproducible (page 54)**. Cover the headline for the article "One Last Ride" before revealing it to students.

2. Read the article together as a class. Ask students to identify the important details and facts within the article. Write the details on the board. Model how to compose three summary sentences based on the details students have identified. Write the sentences on the board.

3. Invite students to review the summary sentences and brainstorm headlines for the news article. Write their headlines on the board, along with the following evaluation questions. Ask students to evaluate their headline ideas.
   • *Does the headline tell what the article is about?*
   • *Does the headline have five or fewer words?*
   • *Does the headline catch the interest of the reader?*

4. Cross out the headlines that do not get a "yes" for each evaluation question. Ask students to vote on the headline they think is most appropriate for the article before revealing the actual headline.

5. After modeling this activity, give each student pair a news story without a headline. Invite pairs to select the most important details about the event and write a three-sentence summary that helps someone who has not read the article to understand what it is about. Then have students use this summary to write an attention-grabbing headline for their news article. Remind them to make sure they can answer "yes" to all three evaluation questions. If not, they should revise the headline.

6. Invite each pair to share their headline with the class. Ask the class to vote on their favorites before you reveal the actual headlines.

# One Last Ride

Coney Island, a strip of land at the southern part of Brooklyn, became a popular amusement park after the Civil War. The first carousel was lighted with kerosene lamps. Musicians played live music. In addition, the hotdog was introduced when Nathan's Famous opened its first stand.

But this summer may be the last time anyone can truly experience the legendary boardwalk at Coney Island. The city is planning to rezone the area. This means that Astroland, along with one of its most popular rides, the Cyclone, will be closing. The Cyclone, built in 1927, is one of the nation's oldest wooden roller coasters. In its place, the city plans to build a glamorous hotel with lots of glitzy indoor attractions.

If you have never visited Coney Island, this summer is your last chance. Grab one last ride on the Cyclone to enjoy those thrills and chills! And while you're at it, grab a hotdog, too.

# Connect to Summarize

The summarizing strategy can take many forms. Making connections between concepts is another way to facilitate summarizing. In this activity, students compare two objects and then write a summary statement that describes their findings.

1. Give each pair of students a copy of the **Connect to Summarize reproducible (page 56)**. Invite pairs to brainstorm a list of functions and characteristics of a cell phone and an MP3 player. Students might create lists such as the following:

## Cell Phone

- Sends and receives calls
- Offers sound and vision
- Stores photos
- Saves messages
- Sends text messages
- Has calendar features
- Has a calculator
- Provides wallpaper and ring tones
- Small and lightweight

## MP3 Player

- Stores songs for listening
- Downloads music and movies
- Stores photos
- Small and lightweight
- Offers sound and vision
- Makes playlists
- Provides games
- Holds album art

2. Have students list the characteristics and functions that the two products have in common in the box labeled *Similarities*.

3. Finally, have students use their list to write a three-sentence summary statement highlighting characteristics that the two products share.

# Connect to Summarize

**Directions:** Brainstorm a list of functions and characteristics of a cell phone and an MP3 player. List how the two products are similar in the box. Then use your list to write a three-sentence summary explaining how the two products are alike.

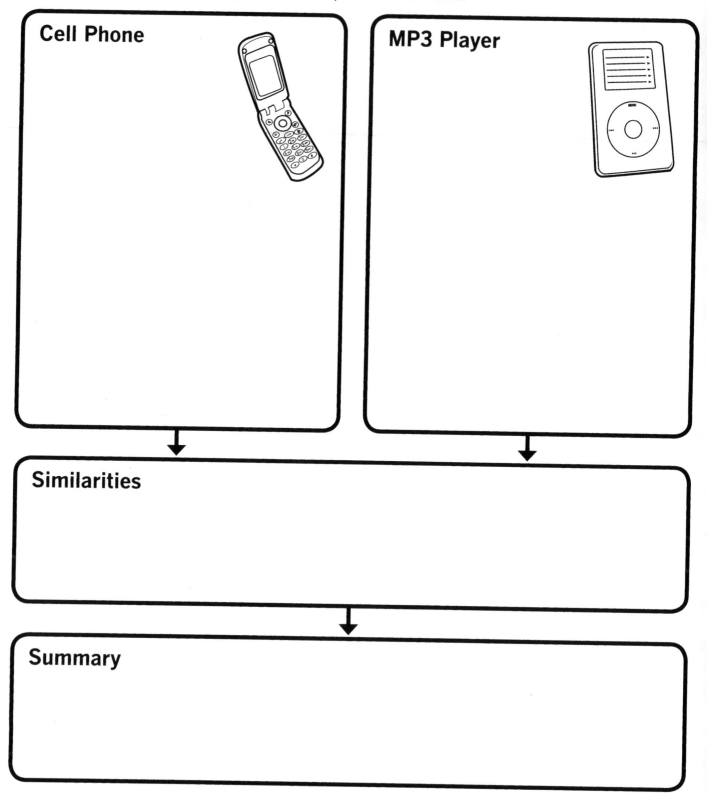

**Cell Phone**

**MP3 Player**

**Similarities**

**Summary**

# Literature Themes

The theme of a story is its "big idea" or message. In fiction, the theme is not presented directly. The reader must extract it from the story's setting, plot, characters, and action. In this activity, students will summarize the characteristics of a story to determine its theme.

1. Before beginning this activity, have students independently read an assigned story and familiarize themselves with the events, plot, setting, and characters.

2. As a class, have students suggest themes for the story. Record their ideas on the board.

3. Then divide the class into groups of three. Give each group a **Supporting the Theme reproducible (page 58)**. Assign each group one of the themes from the list on the board. Have groups complete their reproducibles by skimming the story to find and record details that support their theme.

4. Invite students to share the details they found in the story. As a class, discuss which details are most specific and best support the themes presented. Then ask them to decide which theme they think is most strongly supported.

# I Didn't Know That!

A summary can be produced in a written or graphic format. In this activity, students will use a T-chart to graphically record both familiar and new information.

1. Give students a copy of the **I Didn't Know That! reproducible (page 59)**. Tell them that they will use this T-chart graphic organizer to record what they already know and new information learned while reading an assigned passage.

2. When students have completed reading the text and separating the information into two categories, divide the class into groups of four. Have each group work cooperatively to create a poster with the five most important ideas from each side of their T-charts.

3. Have groups share their posters with the class. Ask them to identify which of the new facts they learned were the most interesting.

978-1-4129-5829-5

# Supporting the Theme

**Directions:** Write the name of the theme on the book cover. Then skim the assigned text to find details that support this theme. Write one detail inside each open book.

**Theme**

**Supporting Detail**

**Supporting Detail**

**Supporting Detail**

**Supporting Detail**

**Supporting Detail**

Name _____     Date _____

# I Didn't Know That!

**Directions:** Write the topic you will be reading about. As you read, write information you already know in the left column. Write new information you learned in the right column.

**Topic:** _____

| I Already Know . . . | I Learned . . . |
|---|---|
|  |  |
|  |  |
|  |  |
|  |  |
|  |  |
|  |  |
|  |  |
|  |  |
|  |  |
|  |  |
|  |  |
|  |  |
|  |  |
|  |  |
|  |  |
|  |  |
|  |  |
|  |  |
|  |  |
|  |  |

# CHAPTER 3

# Monitoring Strategy

Monitoring is thinking about how and what you are reading, both during and after the act of reading. Monitoring begins before the reader actually begins reading the text and continues after the reader has finished reading.

Clarifying is the cognitive partner to monitoring. Clarifying consists of fixing the mix-ups that interfere with comprehension. Some examples of mix-ups that can occur in reading include:

- Confusing characters in a story

- Guessing incorrectly at the meaning of a word

- Not being able to figure out what the author is talking about

- Encountering too many unfamiliar words in the text

- Encountering unfamiliar concepts or ideas

- Getting confused because the text is poorly written

Effective readers fix up their mix-ups in routine and automatic ways, much like skilled drivers adapt to changes in road conditions, detours, or the sense that they are lost. Students who have not yet learned to be strategic or effective readers lack these automatic strategies to adjust to text when it becomes confusing. They lack the skills to maneuver through the comprehension detours and roadblocks that may arise. Monitoring strategies will equip students with the requisite tools needed to navigate demanding text without undue frustration and anxiety.

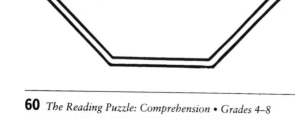

FIX UP YOUR MIX-UPS

# Connecting to Experiences

When reading, students can struggle with unfamiliar concepts because of lack of background knowledge. In this activity, students will learn how to make personal connections to the text.

1. Give students a copy of the **Connecting to Experiences reproducible (page 62)** and make a transparency of it. Explain to students that one effective reading strategy is to connect something they read to something similar they have personally experienced or know about.

2. Read the first text passage aloud to students. Model a personal connection you have with the text by recording a note about it in the box.

3. Invite students to complete the reproducible independently by jotting down a connection they have with each paragraph.

4. Encourage students to use this strategy with everything they read. They need not always write down the connections, but encourage them to make mental notes as they connect to the text.

# Be Word Wise

Content-area reading can be difficult for students because of the many new words and concepts they encounter. In this activity, students will predict the meaning of unknown content-area words and then relate them to their own experiences.

1. Point out an unfamiliar word in a sample text passage and write it on the board. Invite students to predict what the word means by finding clues in the surrounding text.

2. Provide students with a dictionary definition of the word and then relate the word to your own experience. Explain how that connection can help you remember the word and its meaning.

3. Give students a copy of the **Word Wise reproducible (page 63)**. Invite them to use this page while reading to help them predict and identify the meanings of unfamiliar words.

# Connecting to Experiences

**Directions:** Can you make a connection to each paragraph? Read each paragraph and then think about what it reminds you of. Write your connections in the thought cloud.

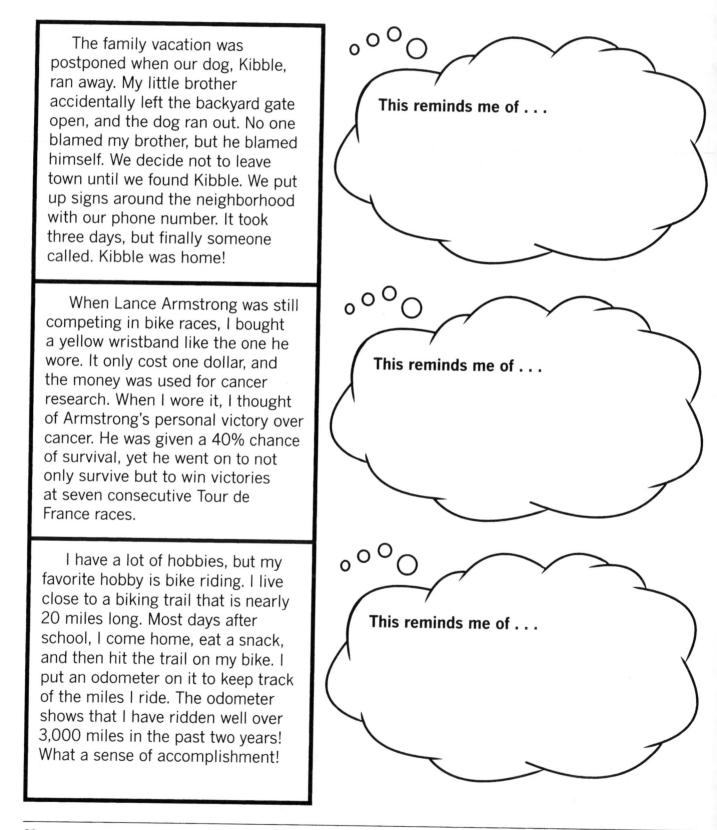

The family vacation was postponed when our dog, Kibble, ran away. My little brother accidentally left the backyard gate open, and the dog ran out. No one blamed my brother, but he blamed himself. We decide not to leave town until we found Kibble. We put up signs around the neighborhood with our phone number. It took three days, but finally someone called. Kibble was home!

This reminds me of . . .

When Lance Armstrong was still competing in bike races, I bought a yellow wristband like the one he wore. It only cost one dollar, and the money was used for cancer research. When I wore it, I thought of Armstrong's personal victory over cancer. He was given a 40% chance of survival, yet he went on to not only survive but to win victories at seven consecutive Tour de France races.

This reminds me of . . .

I have a lot of hobbies, but my favorite hobby is bike riding. I live close to a biking trail that is nearly 20 miles long. Most days after school, I come home, eat a snack, and then hit the trail on my bike. I put an odometer on it to keep track of the miles I ride. The odometer shows that I have ridden well over 3,000 miles in the past two years! What a sense of accomplishment!

This reminds me of . . .

# Word Wise

**Directions:** As you read, write a word in the open book that you do not know or understand. Read the text around the word and predict what you think the word means. Then use a dictionary or glossary to write the actual definition. Finally, write a sentence using the word that relates to your life in some way.

**Word**

Predicted Definition: _____

_____

Actual Definition: _____

_____

Sentence: _____

_____

**Word**

Predicted Definition: _____

_____

Actual Definition: _____

_____

Sentence: _____

_____

**Word**

Predicted Definition: _____

_____

Actual Definition: _____

_____

Sentence: _____

_____

# Word Predictions

When students encounter too many unfamiliar words, comprehension decreases. They can end up feeling confused, and worse, not comprehend what they are reading. In this activity, students will practice making predictions about unknown words by gathering meaning from surrounding context clues.

1. Ask students what they do when they come across an unfamiliar word in a text passage. Explain that the words surrounding an unfamiliar word can provide clues to help them predict the new word's meaning. Write the following words on the board: *impart, insatiable, trilateral.*

2. Ask students if they know the meaning of any of the words. Write students' guesses, or predictions, on the board. Then read aloud the following sentences. Invite students to predict the meaning of each new word based on the surrounding text.
   - *She was able to **impart** her knowledge of the situation to everyone who needed to know.*
   - *My friend has an **insatiable** hunger for knowledge. He never stops learning.*
   - *The United States, Canada, and Mexico have a **trilateral** trade agreement.*

3. Give students a copy of the **Word Predictions reproducible (page 65)**. Have them read each sentence and predict the definition of the boldface word based on the surrounding text. Explain that this surrounding text is known as "context clues."

4. After students complete their predictions, invite them to share their ideas and thoughts. Then reveal the actual definitions.

   **jejune** *adj* **(ji-<u>joon</u>):** juvenile, immature

   **ennui** *n* **(ahn-<u>wee</u>):** dissatisfaction resulting from lack of interest; boredom

   **gregarious** *adj* **(gri-<u>gair</u>-ee-uhs):** fond of the company of others, sociable

   **assuage** *v* **(uh-<u>sweyj</u>):** to soothe, calm, relieve

   **bombastic** *adj* **(bom-<u>bas</u>-tik):** inflated, pretentious, pompous, grandiose

   **heliotrope** *n* **(<u>hee</u>-lee-uh-trohp):** family of plants characterized by leaves that turn toward the sun

   **neophyte** *n* **(<u>nee</u>-uh-fahyt):** beginner or novice

   **virtuoso** *n* **(vur-choo-<u>oh</u>-soh):** person who excels in musical technique or execution

# Word Predictions

**Directions:** Look at the bold word in each sentence. Do you know what it means? Predict the meaning of each bold word based on other words in the sentence, or "context clues." Then use a dictionary to find the actual definition.

| Sentences | My Predictions | Actual Definitions |
|---|---|---|
| **1.** We thought the boys were showing **jejune** behavior because they were acting silly, making strange noises, and cracking stupid jokes. | | |
| **2.** During the long, dry lecture, the students could barely contain their yawns. They wished they could relieve their **ennui** with a snack break or some lively music. | | |
| **3.** Sally is a very **gregarious** person. She is friendly with everyone she meets and makes friends with all types of people. | | |
| **4.** The minister tried to ease the mother's grief when she learned of her son's death. He used kind words to **assuage** the pain she felt from such a terrible loss. | | |
| **5.** The politician was known for his flowery, **bombastic** speeches, which were full of grand promises but didn't offer many real solutions to problems. | | |
| **6.** A sunflower plant is a **heliotrope** because it always turns in the direction of the sun. | | |
| **7.** The student was considered a **neophyte** because he was just beginning to learn how to play chess. | | |
| **8.** At the time of his death, Mozart was considered to be a master of his craft— a **virtuoso** composer. | | |

# Sneak Peek

Giving students a preview of the words and phrases they will encounter while reading is a powerful strategy for increasing comprehension and building background knowledge. In this activity, students prepare to monitor their reading by building sentences with words and phrases they will see in a text selection.

1. To model this activity, write the following words and phrases related to global warming on the board:
   - *greenhouse effect*
   - *gradual*
   - *temperature rise*
   - *earth*
   - *climate*
   - *warmer*
   - *atmosphere*

2. Ask students to make predictions about what the words and phrases mean and to use them in sentences. Write students' sentences on the board. Invite volunteers to look up the words in a dictionary if they think any of them have been used incorrectly. As a group, discuss the definitions and revise sentences if needed.

3. Prepare the **Sneak Peek reproducible (page 67)** for students by writing several words and phrases they will encounter in a reading assignment in the box labeled *Check It Out!* Then give each student a copy of the reproducible.

4. Have students follow the model you presented by using the words and phrases to write sentences. Then ask students to read the assigned text.

5. After they're finished reading, place students in pairs. Have pairs work together to revise their sentences based on new knowledge gathered from the reading.

# Sneak Peek

**Directions:** Look at the words and phrases in the box. Predict what you think the words mean. Use each word to write a sentence. Then read the assigned text. If your predictions were incorrect, look up the words in a dictionary. Then rewrite the sentences.

**Check It Out!**

**Write Your Sentences**

1. _____

   _____

2. _____

   _____

3. _____

   _____

4. _____

   _____

5. _____

   _____

# Metaphor-ize It

A metaphor is a direct comparison of two different things that share a certain characteristic. Or, one thing is used to represent another. In this activity, students will analyze the characteristics of key words and concepts to create metaphors that help reinforce learning.

1. Model this activity by writing a word on the board and asking students to brainstorm its characteristics. For example, if given the word *ballerina*, students might brainstorm words and phrases such as *graceful*, *athletic*, or *beautiful*.

2. Then challenge students to think of something else that shares one or more of those characteristics. In this example, students might name a *butterfly* as also being *graceful* and *beautiful*.

3. Show students how the metaphor *a ballerina is a butterfly* would help them remember the characteristics of a ballerina.

4. Practice creating additional metaphors using the following examples or your own ideas.

    **Term:** cassette player
    **Characteristics:** outdated way to record information
    **Object with a similar characteristic:** dinosaur
    **Metaphor:** A cassette player is a dinosaur.

    **Term:** cell
    **Characteristics:** contains parts that work together
    **Object with a similar characteristic:** factory
    **Metaphor:** A cell is a factory.

5. Give students a copy (or multiple copies as needed) of the **Mighty Metaphors reproducible (page 69)**. Have them use the reproducible to record key concepts and terms they need to remember when studying new material. Invite them to use the steps you modeled to create a metaphor for each concept.

978-1-4129-5829-5

# Mighty Metaphors

**Directions:** As you read, write key words or concepts in the boxes. List some characteristics of these concepts. Then brainstorm an object or concept that has a similar characteristic. Finally, compare the two concepts to create a metaphor.

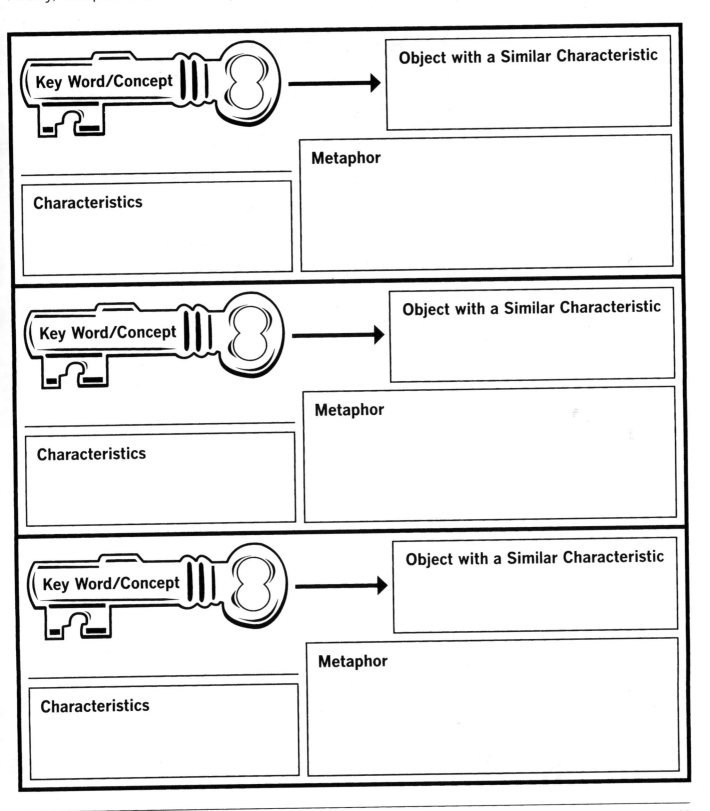

Key Word/Concept

Object with a Similar Characteristic

Metaphor

Characteristics

Key Word/Concept

Object with a Similar Characteristic

Metaphor

Characteristics

Key Word/Concept

Object with a Similar Characteristic

Metaphor

Characteristics

## Monitoring Math Reading

The monitoring strategy involves the ability to think about what you are reading during the reading process. This strategy is especially helpful when students are organizing information about a multiple-step math problem or math word problem. In this activity, students will use a template to categorize information they read in math probelms.

1. Give students a copy (or multiple copies as needed) of the **Making Sense of Math reproducible (page 71)**.

2. Explain the type of information they will write in each box. In the first box, students will write what they know and understand. In the second box, they will draw a picture of what is being asked. In the third box, they will write formulas and equations needed to solve the problem. In the last box, students will write what they think is missing, confusing, or something they do not understand.

3. Invite students to use the reproducible to organize and solve multiple-step math problems and math word problems.

## Monitoring Science Reading

One strategy for monitoring content-area reading is to focus on how ideas are developed. In this activity, students will identify the main idea in text and then focus on how that idea is developed by identifying supporting details.

1. Make a transparency of the **Making Sense of Science reproducible (page 72)** and give each student several copies. Using a sample paragraph from a science text, model for students how to use the reproducible to identify the main idea and supporting details. Write the main idea and the supporting details on the lines inside the beaker.

2. Assign students a paragraph or a chapter to read from their science text. Have them complete the reproducible as they read.

3. After students have read the text and completed their reproducibles, have them share their work with a partner and compare notes. Invite them to use additional copies of the reproducible for future reading assignments.

Name _____                                    Date _____

# Making Sense of Math

**Directions:** Read the math problem. In the first box, write all the facts you know and understand. In the second box, draw a representation of the problem. In the third box, write formulas or equations you may need to solve the problem. In the fourth box, write any part of the problem that you do not understand.

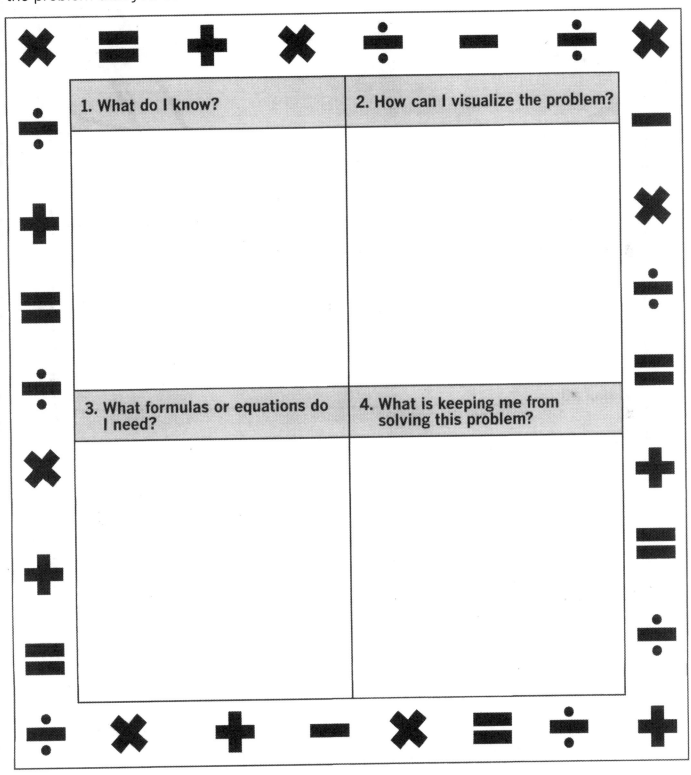

| 1. What do I know? | 2. How can I visualize the problem? |
|---|---|
|  |  |
| 3. What formulas or equations do I need? | 4. What is keeping me from solving this problem? |
|  |  |

# Making Sense of Science

**Directions:** Find the main idea in your assigned text and write it in the top of the beaker. (You will usually find the main idea in the first or second sentence of a paragraph.) Then, as you read the rest of the text, write each supporting detail inside the beaker.

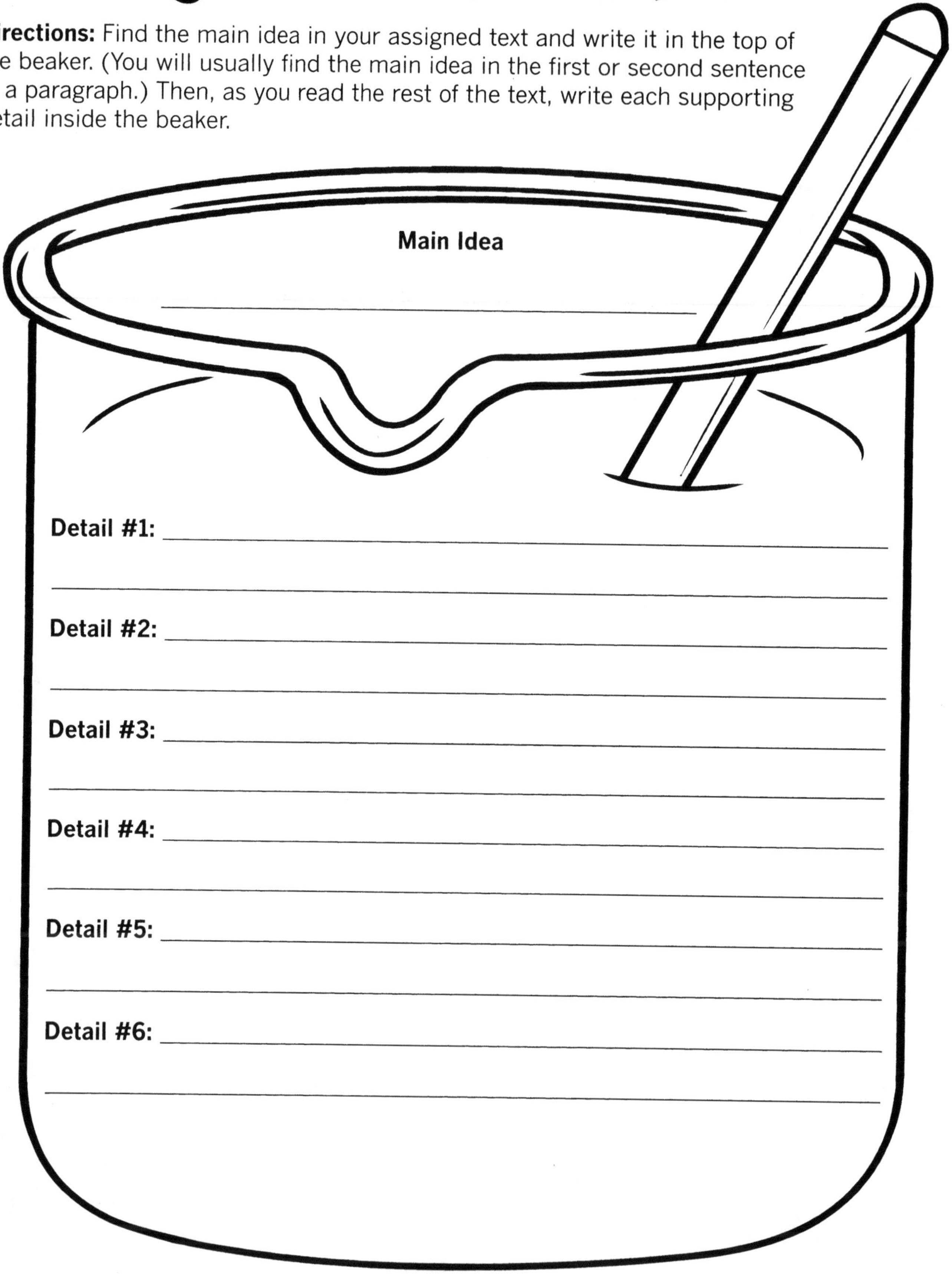

**Main Idea**

_____

**Detail #1:** _____

_____

**Detail #2:** _____

_____

**Detail #3:** _____

_____

**Detail #4:** _____

_____

**Detail #5:** _____

_____

**Detail #6:** _____

_____

# Clicks or Clunks

Skillful readers constantly monitor their comprehension by asking the question: *Is it clicking or clunking?* In other words: *Does the text make sense or not?* In this activity, students will practice identifying information that makes sense to them and information that is confusing.

Click!

1. Make a transparency of the **Clicks or Clunks reproducible (page 74)**. Place it on the overhead projector to model how students will apply this strategy.

2. Use a sample paragraph from a science or social studies text to model how to read, think aloud, and evaluate concepts as either "clicking" or "clunking" in your mind.

3. Record your ideas on the transparency to show students how they can use this strategy to monitor their understanding of text.

4. Give students a copy of the Clicks or Clunks reproducible. Have them use the organizer as they read to record the information that makes sense to them and the information that does not. Remind students to note *why* the information clicks or clunks.

# Save or Delete

Students should understand that everything they read is not of equal value. Some ideas should be saved, while others can be deleted. In this activity, students will monitor their reading by evaluating whether information is important or whether it can be "discarded."

1. Explain to students that main ideas, key concepts, and important facts from text should be saved in their minds. Help them understand that some information is redundant or trivial and can be deleted. Provide students with examples of this type of information using a passage from a textbook.

2. Give students a copy of the **Save or Delete reproducible (page 75)**. Have them complete the reproducible by classifying information they read as material to save or delete. Tell them to write various facts and information in the chart. Then have them go back to evaluate each idea and circle either the treasure chest (save) or the trash can (delete).

3. After students complete the top section of the page and understand the strategy, they need only to record ideas they want to save. Invite them to practice this strategy using the bottom section of the reproducible.

# Clicks or Clunks

**Directions:** As you read, write ideas that make sense, or "click," in the top chart. Explain why the ideas make sense to you. Write ideas that do not make sense, or "clunk," in the bottom chart. Explain why the ideas do not make sense to you.

**Clicks**

| What? | Why? |
|-------|------|
|       |      |
|       |      |
|       |      |
|       |      |

**Clunks**

| What? | Why Not? |
|-------|----------|
|       |          |
|       |          |
|       |          |
|       |          |

# Save or Delete

**Directions:** Write ideas and information from your reading. Evaluate the ideas by circling the treasure chest (save) or the trash can (delete). After you practice this strategy, write only those ideas you want to save.

| Save | Delete | Ideas and Information from Your Reading |
|------|--------|------------------------------------------|
| | | |
| | | |
| | | |
| | | |

**Save!**

# CHAPTER 4

# Organizing Strategy

Organizing involves constructing mental images or graphic organizers for the purpose of seeing the big picture. Being able to see the big picture is an important skill when it comes to organizing large amounts of information. Students must learn how to construct their own "big pictures" so they can easily visualize and remember important ideas.

The benefits of using graphic organizers include the ability to:

- Organize large amounts of information into smaller chunks to make studying easier

- Understand and remember information more readily

- Remember the meanings of new words, including content vocabulary

- Get better grades on tests

- Organize thinking before writing reports and papers

Many types of graphic organizers work well for various disciplines. Word webs, semantic maps, and Venn diagrams are appropriate for language arts concepts. Matrices, flowcharts, and pictures work well for math concepts. Timelines, cause-and-effect charts, and fishbone diagrams work well for social studies concepts. However, when students develop the knack for creating their own graphic representations of text or information, they are truly using their cognitive powers to visualize and organize what they read.

The first step in teaching any strategy is to model it and think aloud for students. Take time before beginning a new unit or chapter to ask students what graphic organizer they believe would be most appropriate to use with the text. Students will quickly begin to see how graphic organizers can reduce cognitive overload by keeping concepts abbreviated, visible, and organized.

SEE
THE BIG
PICTURE

978-1-4129-5829-5

# Fishbone Map

Students can use the **Fishbone Map reproducible (page 78)** to frame their understanding of science concepts or to highlight causes and effects of a historical event. They can also use the organizer to make a visual graphic of narrative text or a newspaper article. For example, students might use the Fishbone Map to outline details about tropical rainforests. They would write *Rainforests* in the *Topic* box and then select six key concepts to write on each of the angled lines. Next, students would search their reading for details that support each concept and write the details on the horizontal lines.

# Word Web

Students can use the **Word Web reproducible (page 79)** to organize information for study. They would choose a word or concept to write in the center box and then write the definition, characteristics, examples, and non-examples in the corresponding boxes.

Emphasize the importance of including non-examples to distinguish between what the word or concept *is* and *is not*. For example, if *crystals* is the key word, examples could be *snowflakes*, *salt*, and *sugar*. Non-examples could be *lava*, *obsidian*, and *coal*. Non-examples show an understanding of crystal characteristics (glassy, clear, sparkling) that they do not share.

# Follow the Sequence

Students can use the **Follow the Sequence reproducible (page 80)** to create a graphic representation of a sequence for:

- Major causes of a historical event

- Events in a narrative

- Steps for a science lab or process

- Order of operations to solve a math problem

When students complete their organizers, they can to share their information in groups and then use the organizers for study and review.

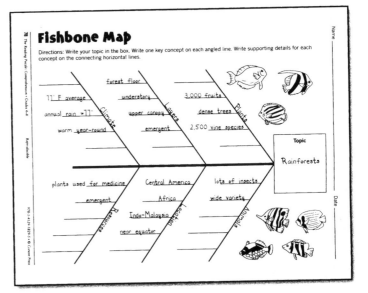

# Fishbone Map

**Directions:** Write your topic in the box. Write one key concept on each angled line. Write supporting details for each concept on the connecting horizontal lines.

Topic

Name _____  Date _____

# Word Web

**Directions:** Write a key word or concept in the center box. Then write ideas related to the key word or concept in the outer boxes.

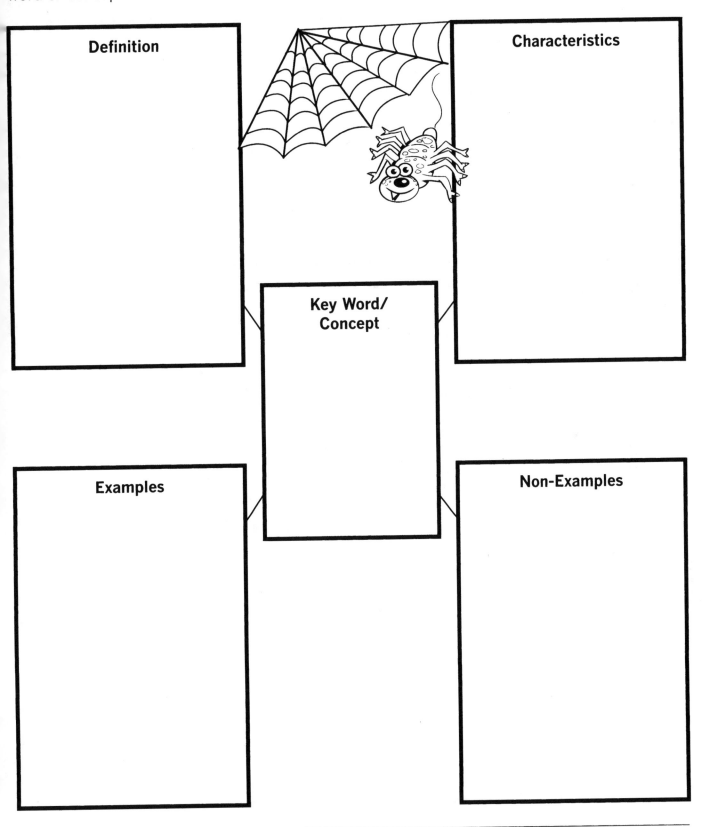

| Definition | Characteristics |
|---|---|

Key Word/
Concept

| Examples | Non-Examples |
|---|---|

# Follow the Sequence

**Directions:** Use this graphic organizer to write a sequence of events, concepts, or steps.

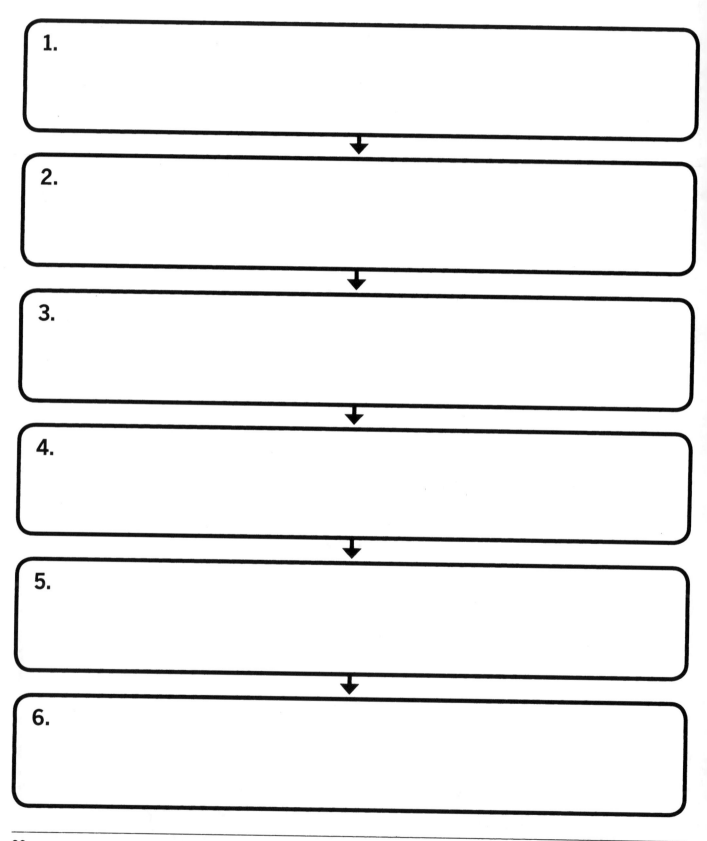

1.

2.

3.

4.

5.

6.

# Finding Similarities and Differences

As discussed previously, comparing and contrasting is an excellent strategy for comprehending text. Students can use graphic organizers to compare and contrast:

- Events in a newspaper article

- Fictional characters

- Events in history

- Science concepts

- Fictional themes or conflicts

1. Invite students to use the **Similarities and Differences reproducible (page 82)** when reading to help them compare and contrast ideas. Encourage students to first focus only on the similarities between the two concepts as they read. Have them jot down their notes on the organizer. Then have them move on to the differences, focusing only on the ways the two concepts are different.

2. After students complete the reading assignment and the graphic organizer, challenge them to draft their ideas into two different paragraphs, each responding to one of the following prompts:

   *How are _____ and _____ similar?*

   *How are _____ and _____ different?*

3. Then have students use the **Compare and Contrast reproducible (page 83)** to simultaneously record both similarities and differences between two concepts as they read.

4. After students complete the reading assignment and the graphic organizer, challenge them to draft their ideas into one paragraph that combines both similarities and differences. Have them respond to the following prompt: *How are _____ and _____ both similar and different?*

# Similarities and Differences

**Directions:** Write two different concepts from your reading. As you read about these concepts, focus only on their *similarities*. Write the ways the concepts are similar in the boxes.

| Concept 1 | Concept 2 |
|---|---|

| Similarities | |
|---|---|
| | |
| | |
| | |

**Directions:** Write the same two concepts from your reading. As you read about these concepts, focus only on their *differences*. Write the ways the concepts are different in the boxes.

| Concept 1 | Concept 2 |
|---|---|

| Differences | |
|---|---|
| | |
| | |
| | |

# Compare and Contrast

**Directions:** Write two different concepts from your reading. As you read about these concepts, focus on both their similarities and their differences. Write the ways the concepts are similar and different.

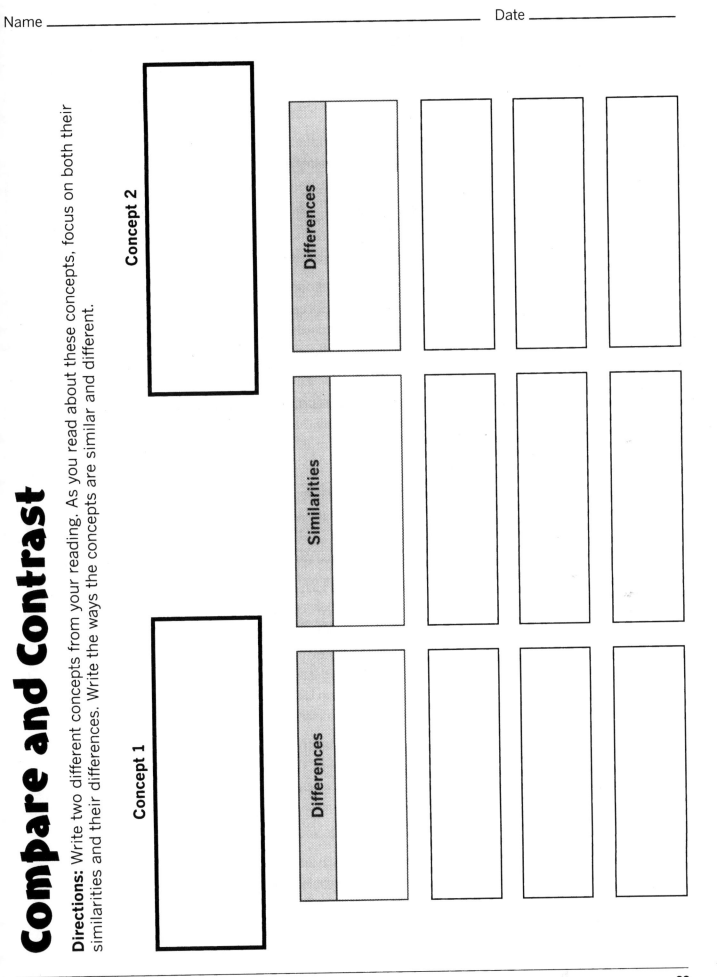

**Concept 1**

**Concept 2**

**Differences**

**Similarities**

**Differences**

# Cause and Effect

Understanding cause-and-effect relationships is essential for reading comprehension. In this activity, students will identify clues in text that point to causes and their effects.

1. Select fiction or nonfiction text that includes clear and distinct cause-and-effect relationships. Use this passage as an example for modeling the strategy for students.

2. Make a transparency of the **Cause and Effect reproducible (page 85)** and give each student a photocopy. After pre-reading the passage and identifying the major event or effect, write it on the transparency.

3. Read the passage aloud to students. Stop and think aloud as you identify clues about the causes of the event. After reading the passage, invite students to identify causes they recall from the passage. Write one cause in each box on the transparency.

4. After modeling the activity, invite students to read a text passage and complete the reproducible independently. After they have recorded their ideas, have students write a paragraph that responds to the prompt: *What caused _____ to happen?*

# Making Evaluations

Evaluating text also includes evaluating characters or people within that text. When students are able to evaluate a character's decisions and actions, they will have a deeper understanding of the text itself. Evaluation helps students to hone their critical thinking skills.

1. Give students a copy of the **Making Evaluations reproducible (page 86)**. Have them use this organizer to evaluate the actions and decisions of two different characters in literature or the actions and decisions made in two different situations in a news story.

2. After recording their ideas about what actions were taken and what decisions were made, have students write a summary statement in response to the prompt: *Which decisions do you think were the wisest?*

3. Encourage students to participate in a classroom debate with others who evaluated the actions and decisions differently.

# Cause and Effect

**Directions:** Write the events or effects you will be reading about. As you read, write the cause for each event or effect.

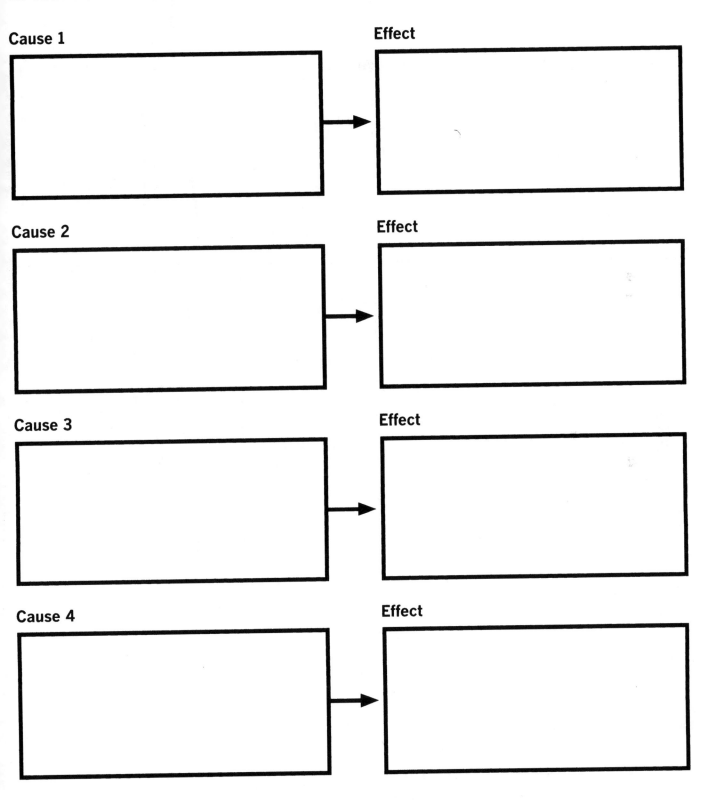

**Cause 1**

**Effect**

**Cause 2**

**Effect**

**Cause 3**

**Effect**

**Cause 4**

**Effect**

# Making Evaluations

**Directions:** Record the actions and decisions of one character or person on the left page. Record the actions and decisions of a second character or person on the right page. Then evaluate the decisions.

**1. Actions and Decisions of:**

**2. Actions and Decisions of:**

**Which decisions do you think were the wisest?**

# Prequel or Sequel?

After students have read an assigned story, invite them to extend their thinking to consider what may have happened *before* or *after* the events they read about. In both instances, students will consider one character and the plot surrounding that character.

1. After reading an assigned story, give students a copy of the **Writing a Prequel reproducible (page 88)**. Ask them to choose and describe one character in the *Character Now* box. Then have students "think backward" and consider what this character might have said or done prior to the story and record these ideas in the *Character in Prequel* box. Challenge them to consider how the prequel character's behavior would have contributed to story events.

2. In the same way, have student choose a plot that involved the character and describe it in the *Plot Now* box. Then ask them to "think backward" again and describe events that may have happened prior to the story's current plot in the *Plot in Prequel* box.

3. When students have recorded their ideas, invite them to write a paragraph that summarizes their hypothesis in response to the prompt: *What do you imagine might have happened **before** the story takes place?*

4. Invite volunteers to share their ideas, explain their thought processes, and point out how the events in the prequel relate to the present story. All the ideas should be connected.

5. On another day, give students a copy of the **Writing a Sequel reproducible (page 89)**. Have them complete this organizer in a similar way by first describing a character and plot from the present story and then developing those ideas further to create a sequel.

6. When students have recorded their ideas, invite them to write a paragraph that summarizes their response to the prompt: *What do you imagine might have happened **after** the story takes place?*

Before Tara moved to New York, she used to ride horses in rodeos.

# Writing a Prequel

**Directions:** Describe one character from the story. Follow the arrow to the left and describe what he or she might have said or done *before* the story. Then describe one plot from the story. Follow the arrow to the left and describe what might have happened *before* the story.

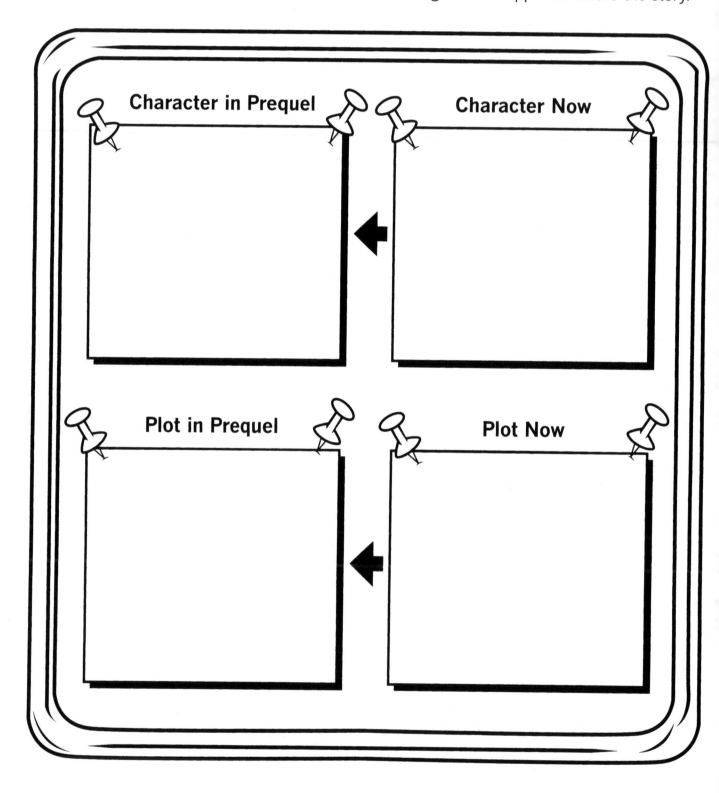

**Character in Prequel**

**Character Now**

**Plot in Prequel**

**Plot Now**

# Writing a Sequel

**Directions:** Describe one character from the story. Follow the arrow to the right and describe what he or she might say or do *after* the story. Then describe a plot from the story. Follow the arrow to the right and describe what might happen *after* the story.

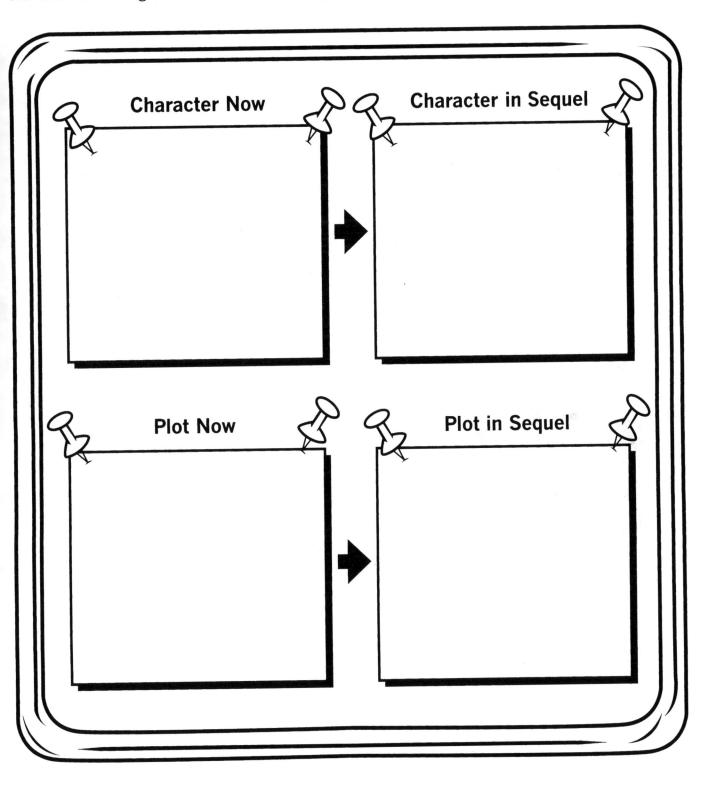

## Picture the Plot

In order to understand what drives a story, students must be able to identify key elements in the plot. Using a graphic organizer can help students isolate and record these elements.

1. Give students a copy of the **Picture the Plot reproducible (page 91)**. Tell them to use the organizer while reading to identify key elements in the plot.

2. Have students begin by writing a one-sentence plot summary in the center box. Then have them write the characters' main problems, decisions, and decision consequences in the corresponding frames. Finally, ask students to explain how the story might have ended differently if the characters had made different decisions. Have them record their ideas in the last frame.

3. After everyone has completed the organizer, have students share their ideas in small groups. Encourage groups to come to a consensus and share their decisions with the class.

## Capture the Character

Similarly, students can use the **Capture the Character reproducible (page 92)** to identify key characteristics and actions of a story's character.

1. Invite students to write the name of one character in the center box. Then have students write the character's physical features, personality traits, actions, and words in the corresponding frames.

2. Have students share their ideas in small groups or pairs. You may choose to pair students who studied the same character so they can determine if they described the character similarly or if they identified different qualities. Or, you may choose to pair students who studied different characters. Challenge these pairs to create a Venn diagram that shows how the characters are similar and different.

# Picture the Plot

**Directions:** Write a short plot summary in the center box. Write the main character's problems, decisions, and decision consequences in the corresponding frames. Then brainstorm a new ending based on different decisions the character might have made. Write your new ending in the last frame.

**Main Problems**

**Major Decisions**

**Plot Summary**

**Consequences**

**New Ending**

# Capture the Character

**Directions:** Write the name of a character in the center box. List at least three details from the story that describes the character's physical features, personality, actions, and words.

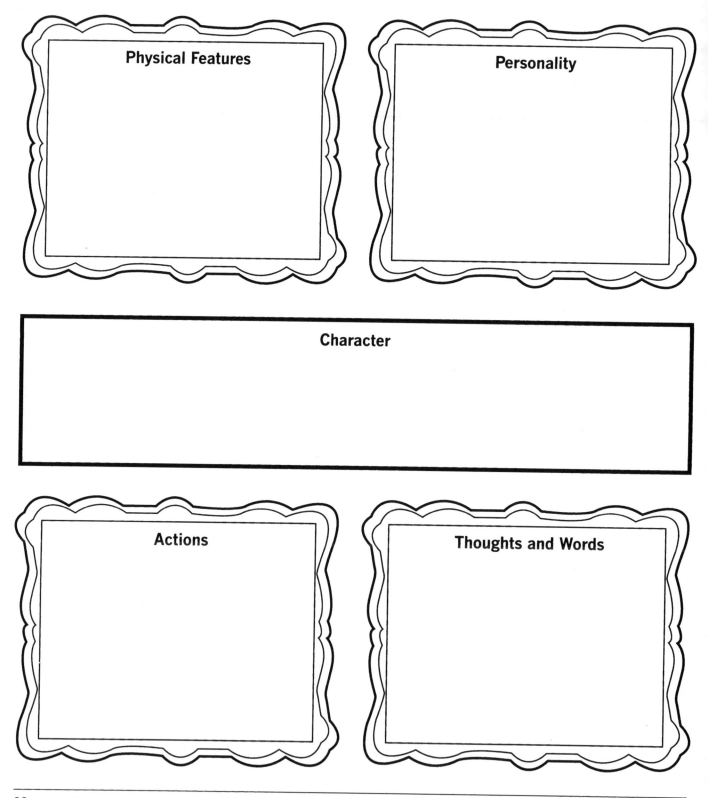

**Physical Features**

**Personality**

**Character**

**Actions**

**Thoughts and Words**

# See the Setting

Further students' understanding and comprehension of story elements by inviting them to evaluate story setting. Remind students that the setting can describe location, weather, time in history, and time of day. All of these elements affect what happens in a story.

1. Give students a copy of the **See the Setting reproducible (page 94)**. Tell them that they will use the organizer to identify and describe the setting in a story.

2. Direct students to briefly describe the general setting at the top of the pyramid. Then have students describe more specific places where the action takes place, the most important features of the setting, and how the setting affects and influences the characters. Have them write their ideas in the appropriate spaces. Finally, ask students to describe changes in the setting that might have altered the story's outcome.

3. Ask students to exchange papers with a partner so they can evaluate each other's work. Then have them share and discuss their ideas.

# Frame Your Understanding

Help students "frame their understanding" of both expository and narrative text by identifying specific elements and recording them in a graphic organizer. Graphic organizers aid comprehension by helping students organize their ideas in a logical way.

1. Give students a copy of the **Frame Your Understanding reproducible (page 95)**. Tell them that they will use the organizer to identify key elements in text. For example, when reading expository text (such as a description of the Boston Tea Party), students might write the following:

   *Who?* American colonists
   *Where?* Boston Harbor
   *Did What?* Destroyed crates of tea
   *Then What?* Sparked the American Revolution

2. After students write a description in each box, invite them to draw pictures in the boxes below that represent their descriptions.

3. Finally, have students write one or two sentences that summarize the information they recorded. Encourage students to use the information from their graphic organizers for test preparation and review.

978-1-4129-5829-5

# See the Setting

**Directions:** Describe the story's general setting. Then, describe more specific locations where the action takes place, setting features, and how the setting influences the characters. Then describe changes to the setting that might alter the story's outcome.

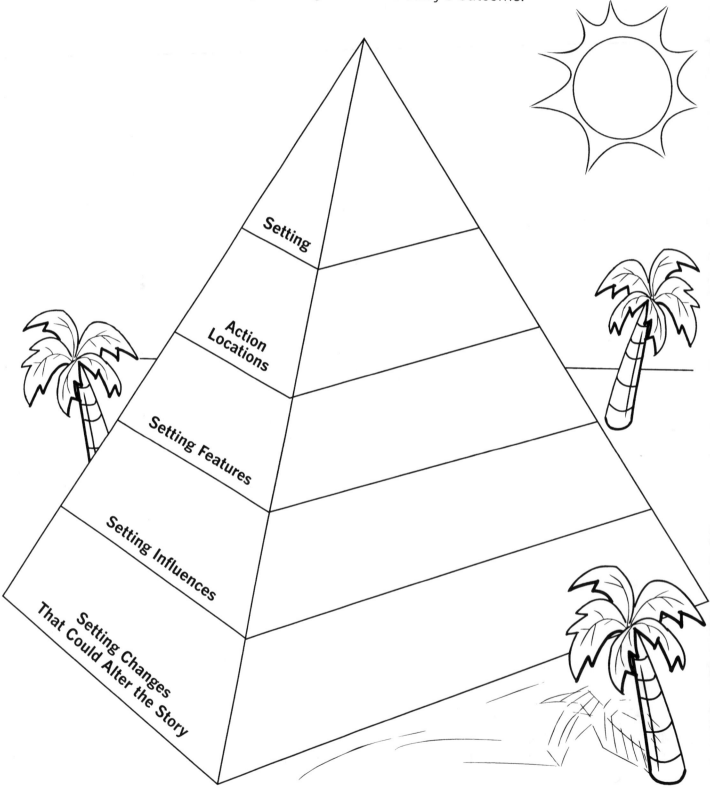

Setting

Action Locations

Setting Features

Setting Influences

Setting Changes That Could Alter the Story

# Frame Your Understanding

**Directions:** Answer each question in the top row. In the bottom row, draw pictures to help you remember the ideas.

| Who? | Where? | Did What? | Then What? |
|---|---|---|---|
| Draw a Picture | Draw a Picture | Draw a Picture | Draw a Picture |

Write a one- or two-sentence summary using the information above.

# References

Baker, L. (2002). Metacognition in comprehension instruction. In C. C. Block & M. Pressley (Eds.). *Comprehension instruction: Research-based best practices* (pp. 77–95). New York, NY: Guilford.

Beck, I. L., McKeown, M. G., Hamilton, R. L., & Kucan, L. (1997). *Questioning the author: An approach for enhancing student engagement with text.* Newark, DE: International Reading Association.

Brown, A. L., & Day, J. D. (1983). Macrorules for summarizing texts: The development of expertise. *Journal of Verbal Learning and Verbal Behavior, 22,* 1–14.

Brown, A. L., Day, J. D., & Jones, R. S. (1983). The development of plans for summarizing texts. *Child Development, 54,* 968–979.

Jones, B. F., Pierce, J., & Hunter, B. (1988/1989). Teaching students to construct graphic representations. *Educational Leadership, 46*(4), 20–25.

McEwan, E. K. (2002). *Teach them all to read: Catching the kids who fall through the cracks.* Thousand Oaks, CA: Corwin Press.

McEwan, E. K. (2004). *Seven strategies of highly effective readers: Using cognitive research to boost K–8 achievement.* Thousand Oaks, CA: Corwin Press.

McEwan, E. K. (2007). *Raising reading achievement in middle and high schools: Five simple-to-follow strategies* (2nd ed.). Thousand Oaks, CA: Corwin Press.

National Reading Panel. (2000). *Report of the National Reading Panel: Teaching children to read: An evidence-based assessment of the scientific research literature on reading and its implications for reading instruction: Reports of the subgroups.* Rockville, MD: National Institute of Child Health and Human Development.

Perini, M. J., Silver, H. F., Strong, R. W., & Tuculescu, G. M. (2002). *Reading for academic success: Powerful strategies for struggling, average, and advanced readers grades 7–12.* Thousand Oaks, CA: Corwin Press.

Shankweiler, D., Lundquist, E., Katz, L., Stuebing, K. K., Fletcher, J. M., Brady, S., Fowler, A., Dreyer, L. G., Marchione, K. E., Shaywitz, S. E., & Shaywitz, B. A. (1999). Comprehension and decoding: Patterns of association in children with reading difficulties. *Scientific Studies of Reading, 3*(1), 69–94.